THE SKILLS OF THE EDUCATOR

DR. WALID KHALID AR-RIFA'I

دار الثقافة
Dar Ul Thaqafah

دار الثقافة
Dar Ul Thaqafah

www.darulthaqafah.com
https://twitter.com/darulthaqafah
Email: darulthaqafah@gmail.com

Find our titles on your favourite online bookstore using the keyword 'Dar Ul Thaqafah'

Translation of the Qur'ān

It should be perfectly clear that the Qur'ān is only authentic in its original language, Arabic. Since perfect translation of the Qur'ān is impossible, we have used the translation of the meaning of the Qur'ān throughout the book, as the result is only a crude meaning of the Arabic text.

Qur'ānic verses appear in speech marks proceeded by a reference to the Surah and verse number. Sayings (Hadith) of Prophet Muhammad (saw) appear in inverted commas along with reference to the Hadith Book and its Reporter.

Contents

Part One

Introduction

All praise belongs to Allah ... thereafter:

When a person possesses a sincere desire to affect those around him, that doesn't necessarily mean that he will accomplish that effect. Rather, it only means that he has taken the first step towards accomplishing the effect!

The desire and ambition are only the fuel that propel the movement of the vehicle. The skills then come to steer this vehicle towards the direction and goal which the driver wishes to reach.

From that which sometimes impacts extremely negatively upon our educating of others, is that we practise the education as a tendency and habitual practice, and not as a skill and science. The matter becomes worse when some believe that putting down principles for educating means complicating it and making it lose its purity, ease, and spontaneity. Perhaps the spontaneous educating of parents and grandparents has been drawn upon to deduce that! Those who think that have been oblivious to the differences in environments, the complexity of requirements, and even, sometimes, some of the negative effects of that spontaneous educating, which mostly taints the student by the educator's reality and not with that which is required! He would then end up being tainted by one colour to another. Indeed, the education styles of the educator himself end up changing in agreeable circumstances in a contradictory manner!

The forthcoming educational points of advice have come to provide mechanisms, visions, and thoughts which the educator would do well to possess in order to assist him, after the assistance of Allah Ψ, to achieve his goal.

And Allah is the One who grants success.

Proceeding in Stages and Gradualism

"Proceeding in stages and in a gradual manner are from the main qualities of the educator. If he was to lose them, he would not be able to be an educator. He would then only be a reformer, conveyor, or someone who commands the good and forbids the wrong."

"The successful educator is not the one who sets the amazing goal. Rather, it is only the one who subjects all his steps and programmes to serve that amazing goal.

"Remember that the provision of water, air and soil is not sufficient alone for the plant to grow. That is because a long period of time is one of the most important of those means, which strengthens the plant whenever it is lengthened and weakens it whenever it is shortened.

"The spike of grain does not need more than a few days for it to sprout, whilst the palm tree requires several years.

"The distinction, great responsiveness, and receptiveness of the student must not lead to rushing through the stages or bypassing some of the doses with him. However, there is no problem instead to provide him with a dose that is greater than that provided to his fellow learners without excess or neglect. Indeed, the life of this world is built upon balance.

"Do not think that it is only the Tarbiyah (educating) which is based upon the principle of preceding by stages and gradually. That is because the whole of life is built upon gradualism, beginning from the creation of the human being and the growth and development of his body and mind, to the revelation of the legislations and rulings. Indeed, even that which was possible to be created by "Be", Allah created in six days!

"The shallow pool of water reveals everything that it contains, whilst the depth of the sea prevents seeing all that it contains.

"Sometimes some things do not attain their effect from the strength of the blows, but rather from their consecutiveness, where time accomplishes that which strength or force cannot. It is exactly like how consecutive drops of water sculpt a solid rock (over time).

"And my Tawfeeq (success and attainment) is only with Allah" ... The educator must have the presence of mind that educating is a work that is undertaken with a human. And as the human fluctuates in respect to nature, temperament, and attitudes, the steps of the educator may not lead to positive results. As such the Tawakkul (trust and reliance) upon Allah must be present, just as the educator must be characterised by having a measure of patience with results which are not good despite all the efforts he has expended.

The Educator's Assessment

"There is no separation between the educating process and the process of assessment. The higher your skills are in respect to assessing, the more precise and accurate you will be in respect to determining the personality of the student and what he needs exactly.

"The importance of assessment lies in it being the ground upon which all your future plans with the student are based upon. When you make an error in assessing the needs of the student, then that means you will waste great efforts in matters that he does not need or in matters that he has surpassed a long time ago. You must remember that understanding the personality of the student is equivalent to setting your footing or the place where your seeds are dispersed. It is upon this premise that its importance is based.

"In the age of internet, satellite stations and open technology, it has become necessary to reduce external monitoring and implant within the student the practise of self-monitoring. That is by making them love Allah and making them fearful of His punishment, in addition to making the student feel responsible for himself:

﴿بَلِ ٱلْإِنسَٰنُ عَلَىٰ نَفْسِهِۦ بَصِيرَةٌ ﴿١٤﴾﴾

«Rather, man, against himself, will be a witness(14)» [Al-Qiyamat: 14]

"Education established upon the basis of authority alone, like that of the family, tribe or state, leads to an outward compliance, which those complying can quickly break away from at the first trial or test they encounter. That is because true education is achieved by internal conviction and not through external fear.

"I believe that you agree with me that the person's inner self (*Nafs*) has its personal sentimental state. It likes and hates, attaches to and averts from. You must therefore not allow these inclinations to act as a judge over your opinions and your assessments of the individuals. If you are someone possessing an impassioned sentiment, you must take the utmost care to make your assessment far removed from personal discretion but rather it must be determined accurately by the facts, realities and accomplishments.

"Some educators are influenced by their own personal inclinations and concerns in their assessments. Consequently, they respond positively to the individuals whose abilities conform to their abilities, and their talents conform to their talents. It is a slippery slope that you can fall into without even realising.

"Those educators who restrict the concept of assessment to critiquing and criticism have fallen into error. The assessment of the student is concerned about developing that which is correct, just as it is concerned with correcting the error. Assessment is therefore not only a process of finding fault, devoid of affirming that which is sound or right.

"Write the name of your son upon a piece of paper and then make two columns. In the first, write the points of weakness which you will attempt to strengthen, and in the second, write the points of strength which you will attempt to make distinguished. Then write the means that you will utilise to accomplish that. In this way our dreams for our children transform into real goals and then into reality, by His permission تعالى.

"You must have a clear and independent examining view in relation to the student. Familiarisation with the opinions of others and consulting them does not mean that you should be held captive by their views and assessments, or that you should become a shadow of them.

"Remember that you are not assessing a stone statue, but rather a living changeable human being. This makes you revisit your assessment of the student from time to time. That is because people can change whilst fixing an assessment may deal injustice to them or to yourself!

"I hope that you are not from those who are influenced by the 'Black or white' principle. They are those who hold that assessment view, which does not see in the one being assessed except pure correctness or pure blackness. People contain many overlapping lines, and the proficient educator is the one who can distinguish between these lines in a precise and clear manner, whilst not relying upon general views to analyse the personality before him.

"Some people suffer from a sharp deficiency in the area of social relations. Let that not prevent you from delving into the reality of this category of people and always remember that many good fruits are covered by a thick bitter skin. That is whilst some of the people possess skills in the arts of communication. Keep these considerations in your mind when you assess and probe the personality of the student, whilst taking care for a misleading appearance to not push you away from penetrating the substance.

"The external environment of the student represents an important arena to understand his personal reality. The external reality here refers to his friends, inclinations and even his prevalent societal norms.

"The background of the one being assessed, or his tribe, family and community, could help you to understand the personality. However, beware of making that your only tool, because, as you know, every principle has its exceptions.

"Do not think that you are able to understand another person through the first meeting, relying upon your discernment, composure and extraordinary ability to know the reality of people. Focus upon the objective measures and sensed matters. That is because it is a tool that is not swayed by emotional or sentimental influence. And do not forget that many first impressions quickly turn out to be ridiculous or quite wrong later.

"To be able to understand others, listen to them more than making them listen to you. And do not be like those who assess others merely through the assessment of their response and interaction with what is put before them!

"If you believe that you are capable of providing an accurate analysis of others without watching them or getting close to them, then you are mistaken. The skilful hunter is the one who watches in wait and carefully draws close to his target before firing his shot.

"The family must deal with the gifted or talented child in a balanced manner. They should not diminish his talent or neglect it, just as they should not go over the top in heaping statements of praise and acclaim upon him, which could lead to conceit and feelings of superiority and arrogance.

"Do not go over the top in acts or statements of motivation before others. That is because sometimes it is not good for the educator to show his extreme admiration or abundant praise for one of his students or children in front of the rest of them. Some may believe that this will motivate them, which has some truth! However, exaggeration in that leads on most occasions to completely opposite results, like despair and concealed hatred, which is directed towards the one being praised as well as the one doing the praising!

The Magnetism or Appeal of the Educator

"Be creative! ... That is because creative thought is one of the qualities of the captivating personality. It means the continuous attempt to treat and develop the current situations to reach the appropriate goal or objective.

"Think positively! ... You will never be a captivating or inspirational educator to others if you complain a lot and continuously grumble. That is as those who possess the captivating personality are always positive.

"Show enthusiasm for that which you want to be done. That is as those who possess the captivating personality ignite enthusiasm towards the work they are undertaking. As such, the teacher who says to his students on the first day of study: "You are about to learn the most important subject you have ever studied in your life", will no doubt capture their hearts throughout the period of the study.

"We may not demand from you to be likeable, intuitive and companiable, as these are qualities which are inbuilt and are not easy to attain. However, on the flip side we do demand from you desist from being unlikeable and unapproachable.

"Accept the people upon that which they are upon without them pretending for the purpose of attaining your acceptance and satisfaction. That is as the people are not (naturally) drawn towards the person whom they make a pretence for his sake.

“Do not expect that you will be captivating merely because you have decided that. Rather, qualify yourself through a good cultural and social background, through good speaking skills, a good stock of experiences or stories, a true practical example and other matters which act as a magnet for the hearts of others.

“When you lose your captivating quality and resort to the use of your authority to influence the one you are educating, you have lost your worthiness to educate. That is because the successful educator is the one who attracts and not the one who imposes.

“The successful educator does not need to call others to appreciate him and his speech. That is as his captivating quality and personality have already fulfilled that task.

“People have an aversion to those who speak a lot about themselves; those who make themselves the centre of the whole world and make of their stories, experiences and lives a text which those being educated regurgitate day and night.

“The one who possesses a captivating or attracting quality, in most cases, is the one who is not preoccupied by his own concerns away from the concerns of others. Rather, he is the one who makes the concerns of others his own personal concerns.

“For the educator to preserve his captivating or magnetic quality and his impact, he must observe the following: To be light in criticism, to possess a light-hearted jovial spirit, to speak about captivating subjects like stories and other such things, to make things straight forward, to praise what is correct a lot, to not speak a lot about personal concerns and to respect the personality of the other even if he is at variance with it or censures it.

"I do not believe that you are from those who think that the seriousness of the educator dictates the absence of joking, just as I also do not believe that you are from those who do not know the way to reach hearts except by making jokes!

"***And I am not from the pretenders***" ... The Prophet Al-Mustafa ﷺ used to admit his mistake, forgetfulness or knowledge of a particular matter, whilst he was the best of creation. That is as the genuine appearance of the personality of the educator upon its true nature without pretence, revealing alongside it something of its errors and deficiency, is considered to be a beneficial area for the student, where he is educated upon: 1) Being realistic in one's view, (2) Discernment in respect to following a model, and 3) Non-partisanship or blind following and support of personalities.

"Be completely sure that all we have guided you to so far in terms of means and styles to attain the captivating or attracting personality does not equal one final single quality and that is: That the educator feels a true and sincere concern, a genuine love and unconditional desire to accomplish something good!

Preparing the General Atmosphere for the Student

"At ease, do not attempt to attack the previous atmosphere of the student until he is relaxed and with you. Delay this step a little, and then he will undertake that by himself.

"Attempt to broaden the circle of relationships to extend it to some of those who are close to the student, like his father, brother or someone else, with the goal of making them not on the opposing side to you, if you were not able to bring them over to your side.

"Be as friendly as you can, but without repugnant pretence. That is because the fake smile in place of the genuine one can cause more harm than benefit.

"The one being educated feeling that he is embarking upon large steps could cause an adverse reaction from him. As such, proceed with ease, calm and complete clarity.

"Before removing some practical hindrances in the reality of the student, seek to remove the non-material hindrances from within him. And always remember that your first area of work is the heart before the reality.

"Preparing the general atmosphere does not mean removing all the inappropriate hindrances, as that may be difficult to achieve. Rather, it means the ability to shape the student in the midst of this bad atmosphere whilst incurring the smallest number of losses.

“Attempt to expand the personal circle of the student and transcend his relationship with you alone, even if you see that this new relationship may not serve your long-term goals, as it represents a link in the (overall) chain of your goals.

“Keep clear as much as you can from infringing upon the red lines of the student when forming the general atmosphere for him. These red lines could be a long-time friend of his, a particular affiliation or his personal inappropriate interests.

“Always remember that preparing the right atmosphere for the student does not mean acceptance of his reality and wrapping it with the cover of legitimacy. Rather, disembarking is required and not surrendering to his reality, following by elevating the student to what you intend for him.

“The length of time in which the student has lived in the general atmosphere may be many years and as such, it would be absolute idealism to think that you can reverse all of that within a few days or weeks!

Addressing the concerns and taking the Inclinations of the Student into Consideration

"The Messenger of Allah ﷺ said: "The most merciful of my nation with my nation is Abu Bakr, and the most severe of them in respect to the command of Allah is 'Umar, the most truly modest of them is 'Uthman bin 'Affan and the most knowledgeable of them concerning the lawful (Halal) and the unlawful (Haram) is Mu'adh bin Jabal ..." The correct education is that which is based upon the correct information. Consequently, are we accurately aware of the ages of our children, their study levels, their points of weakness and strength, their main friends, and their talents?

"The Messenger of Allah ﷺ noticed that Abu Talhah had a loud voice and so he praised him saying: "Verily, the voice of Abu Talhah in the army is better than a thousand cavalrymen (or soldiers)". That is, as he used to use his voice to strike fear into the enemy during the battles. Comment: The successful educator is the one who can discover the talents, however small they may be, and then make something great from them.

"The failures from the educators are those who can only paint one picture in their imaginations concerning what they want everyone they educate to be upon in the future!

"We must understand the personality of the one we are educating before addressing him. The mistake which some educators make is to attempt to make those being educated wear readymade clothing without first making sure that they are the right size for the student!

"When someone knows himself, he is like someone who possesses a map to reach his goals. Therefore, among the greatest matters that the educator can provide to those around him is to accurately define himself and his capabilities. That is because those who do not know themselves well are incapable of correcting the error or developing that which is correct and right.

"The skilful hunter watches his target with precision before firing the shot, and the successful educator is the one who understands well the person he is educating before undertaking the task of addressing him. This goal is accomplished by: Listening well, continuous dialogue, and by establishing a warm, friendly, and close relationship with the one he wishes to address and take care of.

"How great is the error which some educators fall into when they attempt intentionally or unintentionally to produce carbon copies of themselves without paying attention to the points of distinction, distinguishment and difference between them and others.

"It is important for the educator, whoever he may be, to develop the personality of the one he is educating with that which is fitting for his personality and not with that which fits his own personality.

"Did the student provide you his mind and self for you to cancel their purpose or render them ineffectual? If your answer is no, then you must not forget this and allow the student to proceed upon what he likes in respect to that which does not run contrary to your convictions, rather than your likes.

"As conviction and capability increase, productivity and distinction increase ... Do not make your principle with the student be based upon the question: "What are the best areas which he should engage in?" But, rather: "What are the best areas which he likes to engage in, in respect to that which does not oppose your educational goals with him?".

"The advanced and distinguished areas have obscured our sight away from other good areas and fields, even if they appear to be less amazing ... You must take care not to fall into this dilemma when addressing the student, whilst remembering that people represent capabilities, and each is facilitated for what he was created for.

"Remember that the enchanting eye is not everything that the beautiful face contains, even if it is the most beautiful part of it. That is because the beauty of the face is not completed without the mouth and ear, and indeed, even the nose as well.

"Only those with narrow horizons want to restrict all people to one area: Because it is better than others in their opinion!

"Beware that hope causes you to drag the student into an area that he does not proceed well in, just because it is the best area!

"When you misunderstand the concerns of the student and address them, you have done injustice to him by addressing him with that which is not suitable for him, done injustice to the areas of work which he could have undertaken effectively, and done injustice to the tasks that you pushed him into undertaking.

"Knowing the student" ... The task of the educator dictates that he be in front of the student and not behind him. This will never be accomplished if the student feels that the one addressing him does not possess a good vision of the future concerning the future he is directing him towards and the role that he is preparing him for. This requires an accurate knowledge of the student so as to assist him in the role that is suitable for him.

"Clarify the general goal and the specific goal" ... The theme of reformation and guidance is only considered to be a general and loosely defined goal. If we do not outline inside this general theme a defined path for every person we are educating, the results in most cases will amount to nothing and to a lack of focus, even if all of that takes place under the very same banner of reformation and guidance!

"There is no shame to prepare the student for a level higher than your level, and even if it is only in one particular area. That is because this is a natural result due to the differences and disparities that exist in human capabilities and talents.

"What do you want?" ... There is nothing more harmful to the substance of the educational message than the absence of clarity of its features in the mind of the educator. When we do not know exactly what we want from others, what do we then expect them to become?

Instilling Confidence

"Means to instil confidence in children (or students) include: 1) Reducing the number of comparisons, 2) Commendation and praise, 3) Introducing them to guests, 4) Charging him with easy responsibilities, 5) Keeping the secret, 6) Refined social intercourse.

"You cannot construct a high building upon brittle ground, just as you cannot accomplish much from a brittle personality that does not see any value in itself or views itself to be insignificant.

"Our conviction in our own capability to change others and in our capability to change their characteristics, is one of the most important things that motivates us to pursue our efforts with them. That is because when despair seeps into us, where we conclude that the one before us will never change because he is like such and such, we will then stop all attempts at bringing reform or change.

"It may be important for you to elevate the student to behave like an adult, although it may be more important to make him feel that he has really become that. That is because people are not motivated by being adults, but rather it is their feeling that they are adults which motivates them. The person is where he views himself to be placed.

"Beware not be from them... Those educators whose lips do not know the word of praise or commendation, whilst believing that continuously making the people feel deficiency is the best way to encourage them to reach perfection!

"Always remember that a high level of confidence alongside modest capabilities is more beneficial and advantageous than a high level of capabilities with a modest level of confidence.

"We love our children, but do we commend and encourage them? Another question: In our Arab societies how often do our children here words of encouragement and praise, and how often do they hear words of criticism, rebuke, and reproach?!

"Nothing generates confidence like success ... Make others succeed, and even if it is an illusory success that you have created. Then after that, they will succeed with a true and real success, which perhaps you are not capable of producing the like of.

"Do you know who the successful educator is in respect to instilling confidence?

It is that educator who carries the feelings of a father and acts with others like a brother ... These two excellent qualities are what establish sympathy for the student and over his mistakes whilst maintaining appreciation for him and his being. It is from this basis that confidence is instilled.

"Praising what is right can be more important than pointing out the error. That is as many nice actions which others do, may cease to be undertaken by them if they do not find anyone to fortify them within them or to inform them that they are undertaking truly excellent things.

"The person's good view of himself assists him to improve his actions and distances him from the bad actions. That is because he views that they are not fitting of him. This makes us attempt to often use words of encouragement, motivating and lifting confidence, whilst avoiding all what contradicts that.

"'Amr bin Al-'Aas said: "*By Allah, even if lying had been Halal (permissible), I would not have lied, as it is not from the manners of men*" ... Included among the most important matters that we can educate ourselves and others upon is: Respect and appreciation (or valuing) of one's own self. Those who have a positive view of themselves distance themselves from every situation that is not fitting or appropriate for them.

"Fat, skinny, short, from so and so tribe or so and so country, this colour or that ..." Sometimes, the presence of some of these attributes among our children is enough to crush their personalities and create a permanent complex within them, as a result of the criticism of others and their making fun of them. This prompts us to educate or impart in our children the ability to acclimatise with our situations and to have confidence in ourselves.

"The officer shouted at his soldiers saying: "Raise your heads high, O lowly (contemptible) ones!!"

He is indeed and without question a foolish officer; however, he is an example of an oft-repeated image of those who demolish those they are educating and thereafter complain about their weak confidence in themselves.

"We must accept our children as they are, whether they are intelligent or not, or good-looking or not. That is because the non-acceptance of some parents of their children makes them fall short in respect to providing what they need in terms of emotional and psychological support. Some parents may even exaggerate in this regard and begin to classify their children by saying, for example, "This one is his mother's son and this one is my son!".

"Remember that you are an educator and not a police officer!

Even though the educator treats the error, he also develops and builds upon what is right. As for the policeman, then his role is only to deal with errors?

"Use encouragement ... Make the error that you wish to correct a slight matter, and the matter that you wish him to undertake appear easy.

"The Messenger of Allah ﷺ was in a gathering, and a drink was presented to him. On his left there was a boy and on his left were some elderly Sheikhs. So, he said to the boy: "Do you permit me to give to them?" He replied: "No, by Allah, O Messenger of Allah, I would not prefer that my share from you be given to anyone else". And so, he ﷺ gave it to him (i.e. the boy)" ... Comment: On many occasions we may forget that the young possess personalities that must be respected and that our true manners are those which manifest with children before adults.

"The father took out a new 100 Riyal note and said to his children: "Who wants this?" They all then raised their hands. He then began to crease and crumple it up with his hand. He then asked again: "And now, who wants it?" So, they all raised their hands (again). He then threw the note upon the ground and crush it with his foot and asked: "And now?" They then repeated their wish to have it. The Father then said: "Just as the value of money doesn't change, likewise, however much you are subjected to disparagement and insult, your true value will not change as long as you are truly confident in yourselves".

"Napoleon was asked: "How do you provide confidence among the individuals of your army?" He said: "Whoever says: "I cannot", I say to him: "Make an attempt". And whoever says to me: "I don't know", I say to him: "Learn". And whoever says to me: "Impossible", I say to him: "Give it a try".

Communication Skills with the Student

"Make your image as good as possible, but beware not to manifest an image other than your true image, as you will not be able to continue upon that. The requirement is to improve and develop your own true image and not to act out an image that does not actually exist!

"The opposite result" ... It is very important that we appear before those we are educating as we are, without undertaking deceptive processes of beautification upon our personalities, which leads to negative reactions from our children and students after the true reality is revealed. 'Umar bin Al-Khattab said: "We have been forbidden to pretend".

"It is important that the student feels the presence of concern for him. However, beware that exaggeration in that can lead to opposite results to those intended.

"Interact with the student with the consideration that you can also benefit from what he has. In this way you will get him to attain a greater benefit from you. That is because the feelings attached to giving are from the main means to facilitate acceptance and benefiting from others.

"Make your goal (ever) present before you and do not allow daily practises and confusions to be a reason for the dilution of your goal or its lack of clarity, leading the student to enter a circle that you intended to extract him out from!

“Make your cheerful disposition and good companionship an alternative and source of relief for what the student may find from you in terms of burdens he is responsible to discharge of. If, however, you wished to combine the weight of responsibilities with the burdens of the self, then your educating of him at such a time will not be effective.

“The educator must precisely know the major and main issues that he wishes to implant in the one before him, so that he can repeatedly deal with them with a variety of different means and ways, and so that he does not lose sight of those major issues in the ocean of minor daily points of guidance.

“I do not believe that you are from those who think that the seriousness of the educator dictates the absence of laughter, just as I don’t believe that you are from those who do not know any path to reach the hearts besides laughter.

“For you to reach your goal accurately: You must improve some of your skills of communication and make them serve your goals. These include: The arts of dialogue, convincing, suggestion, listening, and similar skills.

“The word 'connection or communication' contains within its meaning something about a mutual relationship. For this relationship to be successful: Take extra care not to be someone who only exports (or gives out), as your relationship only grows and develops through importing (or taking in) some of what the student has as well.

“When someone came to the Prophet ﷺ asking or requesting something from him, he would turn to face him” Sahih Al-

Bukhari. Look at the face of your child when he is speaking. Research has proven that the words which are said only transmit 20% of the meaning intended to be delivered, whilst the remaining 80% of the meaning is transmitted through facial expressions and body language.

"Elevate the student higher and beware that he does not descend with you ... A soldier said to his officer at the time of his graduation: "Sir, I have not seen an officer who is as good at speaking with the soldier as you lot. You speak to him as if he is an officer like yourselves. I have seen many officers attempting to imitate you, but they go about speaking with the soldiers as if they had become soldiers like them! And this is the crux of the error itself!"

"The first link in the chain only" ... Often the educator descends to the level of the student with his thoughts, concerns and interests and not the opposite, where he raises them to his level ... There is no doubt that the solidness of the relationship is an important condition to have an impact or influence, however, it only represents the first link which must be followed by other links in a long chain of giving direction and having an impact.

"The optimistic educator transmits his optimism to the student and participates in transforming him into a positive person. That is as the pessimistic one is a demoralised person, who complains often, works little, despairs quickly and in most cases does not have a goal for himself.

"Utilising the problems" ... The problems should be considered to be from the positive means of having an impact upon the student. That is where they are regarded to represent an opportunity for solutions and stances which natural and calm atmospheres do not provide. They may provide a more powerful impact than the instruction that is detached from the realistic current problem ... For example: “The problem of the Ansar with the Prophet Al-Mustafa ﷺ in relation to the distribution of the spoils of war”.

“Age is not an obstacle” ... In the Seerah (biography) of the Al-Mustafa, the Prophet ﷺ, and his noble companions, we notice that there was a large difference in age between them. Despite that, it did not represent an obstacle in respect to the exchange of points of guidance. That is because the true disharmony does not arise from the time or age gap which separates the educator and student, but rather arises from the mental and emotional gap that exists between them.

“Education between two generations” ... The age difference between the educator and the student is not considered in itself to be an educational problem. Rather, the problem lies in succumbing to the effect of this difference in age, in relation to not understanding the needs of the age of the student and his way of thinking. This manifests in the relationship between parents and their children where the age gap between them is wide, and consequently each party comes to represent a different generation.

“Understanding the student is the path to educate him” ... In order to lighten the impact of the age gap between the educator and the student, it is necessary to understand the special features of the age stages for every age group and to be able to read them, in addition to reading the reality which the student lives and what it carries in terms of different newly occurring realities from those experienced by the educator in the previous time period. This makes him more understanding of the needs of the student.

"Turning a negative into a positive" ... Sometimes the age gap between the educator and student is in the interest of the educational process, in the case where the level of readiness to accept and receive increases alongside the increase in the age gap, just as many of the problems associated to sharing a common age between the two parties are removed.

"The secret behind making real impact" ... The readiness of the student to accept and respond to the educator is directly linked to the educational, social and cultural abilities of the educator, and before that, the characteristics which are worthy of being emulated and followed. The age gap, the social and material situation, and what resembles these are influencing branch factors, but they are not conclusive.

"Quick meals (or fast food)" ... The abilities of educators vary greatly in terms of capacity and the spirit and time levels are often less than the needs of the students. For that reason, the educator is sometimes in need of quick meals through which he envelops the largest number of his students or children as possible, which can be reflected in: The passing word, the small gift, the kind commendation, quick consultation, short message or clever message.

“Be appropriate in your appearance: Taking care of the fundamentals does not mean neglecting the appearance. That is because some may make a connection between the two and at the first stages of the relationship in particular.

The Good Relationship and Amiability

"Your good connection with the student represents your stock in him, through which any deficiency, point of aversion, error or trouble in your relationship with him can be overcome.

"Do not cast your seeds until you have prepared in the heart of your companion a suitable place to plant them, so that it can continuously yield its fruit by the permission of its Lord.

"The successful educator is the one who considers establishing the good relationship and amiability as part of his goals. It does not only represent a means to achieve his goals alone, but rather with that goal he accomplishes a whole host of other goals which may not be accomplished without it.

"There are few people who can stomach eating a particular food, regardless of its quality, from a dirty table and filthy plates. That is because good fundamentals do not eradicate the need for also maintaining a good appearance.

"Think about the one you are inviting before you ask him to think about your invitation. Only at that time will he feel that he is a part of your invitation and concerns. He will then share with you in the invitation, in the case where he has become both one of its invitees and one of its patrons at the same time.

"The good relationship with the student may demand forming the good relationship with those around him as well. That is because just as people love themselves, they also mostly love everything that is special to them and belongs to them.

"Do not make your stock which you draw from in your relationship with the student based on the standing of the teacher. Rather, add to that stock through the relationship of amiability and affection. After that, he will award you that position of honour.

"The successful educator is the one who can win the heart of the student through numerous and various forms, like the smile, word, gift, humour, friendly wrangling, keeping the secret, giving responsibility, relieving his anxiety, assisting him with his problems and by not reprimanding or insulting him.

"O Messenger of Allah, verily I love so and so person" "Have you informed him?" "No". "Go and inform him" ... We are often very reluctant to mention the sentiments of love for those we love and conceal those sentiments inside our hearts. That is whilst people love to hear the word love and even if they have heard it before. Just as they love for it to be continuously reaffirmed and for it to be demonstrated in various ways.

"Education derives its impact from love and the statement "I love you" opens the path to every educational message that you address. It was related from Mu'adh (bin Jabal) that he said: The Messenger of Allah ﷺ took hold of my hand and said: "I love you O Mu'adh". I said: "And I love you O Messenger of Allah". The Messenger of Allah ﷺ then said: "So, do not forget to end every prayer by saying: My Lord, assist me upon remembering you, being grateful to you and worshipping you in the best manner".

"'Ali bin Abi Talib described the gathering of the Messenger of Allah saying: "He used to give every one of those sitting with him his share, in the case where each one sitting with him would think that there was no one being more honoured than him". In this way, none of his companions felt that someone other than him was closer to the heart of the Prophet than him. Comment: The ability of the educator to show his concern and positive feelings towards others and making every person feel special, provides him with perfection in manners and power in respect to producing an effect.

"The Prophet ﷺ used to bring his knees to the knees of the one he was speaking to, he used to place his hands upon the thighs of the one he was speaking to, and he would give him his full attention. It has been proven now that the mere touch makes the sensation of affection and warmth of relationship be raised to the highest levels. Therefore, if you wish to talk to your children or advise them, draw close to them with your heart, body and feelings.

"The person's need for love and appreciation does not cease and it increases when we rectify his mistakes. We need to reassure him that his error has not negatively impacted upon his great value in our hearts.

"All fathers love their children but do the children feel that love? And are we successful in expressing our love to our children by making real time for them, playing with them, listening to them, encouraging them and showing them respect.

"A major error which some educators fall into is when they believe that the need for establishing good amiability and a good relationship is restricted to the initial invitational stage, whilst the educational process after that can do without that!

“Many students find it enough from you, in respect to establishing a good relationship with them, that you receive them well, in terms of the things they say, their concerns, complaints and indeed, even their witty comments and jokes.

“I do not believe that you are from those kinds of educators who make overbearing strictness their motto, where they think that smiling, laughing and being sociable with the student impairs them and the educational process as a whole?

“Joking and using light-hearted humour are from the important means to have an impact upon others. The “stiff or emotionless” father or educator is the one who has a weak impact. We can deliver many of the principles that we wish to deliver via humour, joking, and the light-hearted comment. That is as the life of the Messenger ﷺ included purposeful humour.

“The Messenger of Allah ﷺ said: “*Verily, Allah loves the household, in which gentleness (or kindness) has entered*”. Some parents believe that as long as their children’s fear of them increases, it is evidence for their success and strength! The truth (however) is: That the successful educator is the one whom his children and students love and not the one whom they fear!

“He ﷺ said: “Kindness (or gentleness) does not exist in anything except that it adorns it, and it is not taken away from something, except that it leaves it defective” ... When our sternness with others makes them scared of seeking our counsel and expressing their personal affairs to us, that is an indication that we have moved away from the commendable strictness to the abrasiveness that is dispraised.

"The mutual relationship" ... It is beneficial for the educator to make his student participate with him in some of his ongoing concerns or his moments of celebration and sadness, or to consult him in some matters related to him. In addition to what this produces in terms of a warm relationship, it represents a fertile arena to educate through occurrences and circumstances. Just as it provides a demonstration of the life of the educator just as it is without pretence or feigning, where the true and natural dimensions of the example or model become numerous.

"Education is not a job" ... The warm relationship built upon love and respect cannot be demonstrated or fulfilled like a job in a particular time and place ... Whoever looks down on the one he is educating is not suitable at all to be an educator, even if he was to feign love and humility. That is because the deep-rooted characteristics of the self cannot be hidden behind behaviours of pretence, whilst the factor of time is sufficient to expose the natures of people and their true realities.

"Ruining the education" ... In educational work (in the house, nursery or school), the strained and aggravated relationships are considered to represent the easiest way to poison the educational atmosphere as a whole and to completely kill the educational process. Whilst, on the other hand, building affection and friendship with the student represents the first step towards building and elevating him.

The Conviction

"The successful educator requires the ability to convince the other party and not the ability to compel him.

"First believe in your idea: Believe in it to the level of the ardent belief ... Then, at that time alone, make others believe in it!"

"You may be good at showing an argument to be false, however, that does not mean that you are also good at convincing. There is a major difference between convincing and refutation, however, the problem is that many who practise refutation believe that they are actually undertaking the task of instilling convictions.

"Don't think that your task ends by merely casting what you have upon the ears of the student. That is because it is easy to lead the horse to water, however, it is difficult to make it drink from it.

"It is not possible to produce a creative person or someone of high aspiration from someone who is unconvinced of what you want from him.

"The harsh heart could frighten the students and make them of those who are submissive and bow down, even if they are not convinced ... However, I do not believe that you would accept working with slaves for the purpose of serving a sacred goal?

"Convince the student of everything that you wish and demand from him, and when you see that it is best not to reveal to him the wisdom behind what you want from him, then convince him also of this matter. That is because unjustified instructions kill the student and do not develop him.

"Consulting the children (or students) develops their minds and it increases their closeness to us in addition to our understanding of them. It is also a means to convince them of what we want and to make us contented concerning what they want.

"The best means to convince the student is to sprinkle experiences upon him which is a unique style employed in the Qur'an. Take great care as much as possible for those experiences and stories to be close and related to the current time. That is because the closeness of time is one of the important influencing factors in respect to the convincing process.

"Acknowledge the mind of the student and beware of making it redundant through your exaggeration in respect to demanding unwarranted submission to what you want, due to you merely being greater than him in terms of mental capacity and more experienced than him. That is because if you were to deal with him in this manner, from where then would he attain the discerning mind and rich experience?!

"The mistake of compelling the student, even upon what is correct, could be greater than the error of convincing him of a particular action, even if it was incorrect. That is because the person who proceeds upon other than sufficient conviction would quickly cease his procession due to the least of obstacles that he encounters.

"Make use of the sensed material things to present the theoretical idea which you want the student to become convinced of. Providing the girl with a choice, for example, between two sweets, one of which is wrapped and the other revealed, followed by her natural choosing of the wrapped one, has a greater effect in terms of convincing her than one hundred exhortations that she hears about the virtue of wearing the Hijab.

"Who is it that created for you your sweet eye? Who created for us chocolate and sweets? Who made us grow up and cured us (when we were ill)?" ... In this manner we cultivate the love of Allah inside our young children and not by making them memorise it by saying "I love Allah".

"The mother wants her son to bathe but instead of commanding him directly to bathe she makes him feel his freedom and individuality by saying to him: Do you want to bathe before or after the evening meal? The son answers and chooses one of the two choices and then feels that the choice to bathe was his own and not something he was coerced into!

"To convince others of what you want, you must be completely convinced of what you want. That is because the thoughts which are uncertain within people, cannot be made to be firm within others.

"Do not convince others based on your voice being louder, your status bigger, or the inflection of your voice being sterner and sharper. Rather, let it be because your argument is stronger and clearer.

"Cooperation between the educator and the student in respect to undertaking any matter is better than tens of abstract instructions and exhortations to him. That is because forming a close association and living interaction increases the closeness of the student to the educator, just as it increases the educator's understanding of the student.

"The cheerful personalities are closer and have a greater ability to convince others than other personalities. The use of friendly humour breaks the psychological barriers and increases the openness of others to respond and to be influenced with complete ease and peace of mind.

"Beware not to use your speaking skills to convince someone else of something wrong just because you want to escape from an embarrassing situation or a particular discussion. If you were to do that, then perhaps you would have succeeded to escape from that situation, but only after having lost the standing (or dignity) of being an educator in the eye of the one you are educating.

" There is a low style that some of those presiding over education may fall into. It resembles what is known as "arm-twisting", where those educators employ their good will towards the one being educated as a means to apply pressure upon the convictions, decisions and situations of those they are educating.

"Lack of clarity is the path towards (negative or false) suppositions" ... Lack of clarity from the educator or the one being educated means that the message exchanged between them will not be fulfilled in the required manner! People have become accustomed to not fill the distances of obscurity existing between them with positive thoughts or good suppositions.

"A deceptive Aura" ... On some occasions, some educators adopt a level of obscurity in their personalities. Through that the educator gains a certain amount of awe (or respect) and gives the impression of some level of depth. However, these are temporary manifestations which quickly disappear with the passing of time.

"Between obscurity and clarity" ... From among the reasons which motivate the educator to adopt obscurity in his positions is his inability to explain the reasons for the positions he undertakes! And when we clarify the dimensions of the decisions and positions he takes, then this 1) Improves the notions, 2) Increases the driving force towards them and 3) Eliminates the semi-obscurity in the dimensions of these decisions from the start.

"Negative educating" ... We may exaggerate in testing the level of the compliance and responsiveness of our students and children through directions (or instructions) which are unjustified and unconvincing to them! However, the educator does not want to produce followers, but rather capabilities possessing competency ... If Allah, Glorified be He, the Highest, the One to whom belongs the entire command (and affair) and the absolute and unrestricted compliance, Glorified be His Majesty, has explained the reasons for some of the Islamic legal rulings, then what about the case in respect to human directions (or instructions) which are susceptible to being either correct or incorrect?!

Living interaction (is the quintessence of the educator)

"Educating (Tarbiyah) is not a university study completed from a distance or by remote control ... The first condition of education is live interaction and forming a close association. When parents do not give time to their children, then their hopes in respect to rectifying their children will never be anything more than muddled dreams!

"Education is live interaction and close contact" ... Forming a close relationship, sociability and live interaction are necessary in education. The educator does not deliver his message by control from afar. This was the course followed by the Prophet ﷺ with his companions. That is because he did not characterise them as being his students or followers, but rather as his Sahabah (companions), derived from "Suhbah" (companionship).

"Education is not a magic word we deliver which then directly changes the conduct of the student. Education is continuous direction, constant pursuance, precise observation, allusion and clear statements, gentleness and strictness, mixing and live interaction, offering and gifting, patience and perseverance, and overlooking and turning a blind eye. Then it is a matter of Tawfiq (success and attainment) granted by Allah Glorified be His Majesty.

"The Prophet ﷺ use to sit after the Fajr prayer and ask who had a vision (in a dream), so that he could interpret it for him" ... Comment: The role of the educator is not limited to only providing advice and direction. That is because the successful educator is close to the life of the people, their needs and concerns.

"The most dangerous of moments in the relationship of a husband and his wife is when one of the two parties is convinced that there is no point in dialogue or discussion to take place between them. That is because at that time divorce will represent the only way out for them.

"The Prophet ﷺ said: "*Comply with one another and do not differ amongst yourselves*" ... Marital life is not a perpetual life of happiness and bliss, and if both husband and wife do not compromise somewhat from their innate natures, convictions and thoughts, then the married life between them may not endure.

"The husband and wife treating each other well is not only behaviour driven by the love and affection existing between them. Rather, it is also a great act of worship through which both of them draw closer to Allah. The Prophet ﷺ said: "*The morsel (of food) that you place in the mouth of your wife contains a reward for you (from Allah)*".

"The marital disagreements which take place in front of the children have a bad and negative impact upon their psychological dispositions and it may cause them to take sides with their mother against their father, or the opposite. It also diminishes their kindness (or good treatment) and respect towards their parents firstly and then towards their brothers and sisters secondly.

"The first step towards correcting our children is to make right that which exists between us and our spouses. That is because the effects of the shaky relationship between the husband and wife extends directly and indirectly to their children.

"The married couple may run away from confronting their problems thinking time is sufficient to solve them. However, in most cases what happens is that time increases them and, in the end, they could be compelled, after long suffering, to face that which they had been running away from!

"The father being preoccupied away from his children increases the probability of exposing them to antisocial behaviour or criminality. This is a heavy tax that children pay without parents even being aware of it!

"The child accompanying his father increases his social capabilities and self-confidence. We must not fall short in that out of fear that our children will embarrass us by their mistakes in front of others. Indeed, Al-Hasan and Al-Husain used to come to the Prophet Al-Mustafa ﷺ whilst he was giving the speech. He would then interrupt his speech and kiss them, before returning to it.

"The role of the father and his duties must not be practised by anyone else in the household, even if that was by a brother or uncle. And when we go too far in respect to delegating the oldest brother to undertake the role of the father with the rest of his siblings, that could ruin more than what it fixes. A sensitiveness or negative impact could then arise amongst the siblings which is difficult to remedy.

“A servant is meant to assist the wife in housework; however, the calamity occurs when she turns into a second mother and in some cases, the primary mother!

“The woman working intensively during the early years of the child’s life produces children who are introverted, aggressive and behind in their studies and all of that is not realised by us except after it is too late!

“There have been many warnings concerning the danger of the servant undertaking the Tarbiyah (educational raising) of the children. However, the conclusion of all those warnings is: That the mother must remember well that the role for the purpose of which this woman was brought to undertake was that of being a “servant” (or assistant) and not a “mother”.

“A study undertaken upon a number of children who live with their mothers in social prisons established that their psychological and emotional stability is much greater than those children who live with servants more than they do with their “nominal” fathers and mothers!

“The results of a questionnaire covering 2.5 million French women concluded that 90% of women prefer staying in their homes and not going out to work. They said: “We have become fed up with equality with men and we have become fed up with the life of day and night restlessness and waking at dawn to run after the train. We have become fed up with marital life where the husband does not see his wife except at the time of sleeping and where the mother does not see her children except at the dinner table!”

"A study under the heading "Mothers and the cessation of observance" indicated that 70% of the psychological problems of children and teenagers are a result of the mother fleeing from her responsibilities towards her children whilst casting them off to the servant and that the mother's distance stands as a high wall preventing the progression of their children and their development.

"At a time when many of our women cast their role in the house upon the shoulders of the servant, some studies mention that women in the most developed country of the world "Japan", take responsibility themselves of all the affairs of the house, in terms of raising and educating their children, managing the affairs related to living and even paying the bills, amongst other matters!

"Family meetings are an opportunity to exchange experiences in respect to the ways of educationally raising the children, just as they represent an opportunity to rectify some of the common errors of those people who are close (to us) from those we know and are aware of the errors they make with our children.

"To know who is really educating your children, ask yourself this important question: How many hours do I sit with my children? And how many hours do they sit in front of the television or computer?

"Sometimes the child may be deprived of the feeling of the presence of his parents, even whilst they are living. That is because the father is always busy with his work whilst the mother has delegated her tasks to the servant. In truth they are imaginary parents. Indeed, people may pay attention to the orphan due to his being an orphan whilst none are taking notice of those deprived children!

"If the father was to calculate the periods of time that he is absent from his home due to work, travelling or his social interactions, he will realise how little time he is spending living with his children! Just as he will realise how much he needs to invest these times with them in the best of manners!

"All educational and raising convictions and principles which we learn lose their real value when we are occupied away from sitting with our children. There is no benefit in possessing an excellent electronic device if you don't have electricity to make it function.

"Our aspirations and goals for what we want our children to be in the future must correspond to what we present to them in terms of effort and time in the present. Otherwise, our aspirations will turn into nothing other than daydreams!

"At work you are a person of major responsibility and a person of high standing. However, your children at home want you as a loving and simple father. Jabir said: I entered where the Prophet ﷺ was and he was walking on his hands and knees while Al-Hasan and Al-Husain, may Allah be pleased with them both, were riding upon his back and he was saying: How delightful is the camel, your camel, and how delightful a load you two are".

"The Tarbiyah (raising) begins from the beginning of the pregnancy, in the case where medical science has confirmed that the nutritional intake of the mother during the pregnancy reflects upon the foetus in her womb. Just as her exposure to pressures and problems makes the child susceptible to being irritable and quick tempered.

"The events occurring around us represent a golden opportunity for educating and impacting. That is as many of the instructional and educational Ahadeeth of the Prophet ﷺ were said in relation to a situation, a response to a question or to make use of an incident. That is because Tarbiyah (educational raising) is an integral part connected to life and not something that is separated from it.

"As we are not able to prevent our children from making personal contact with bad people or negative influences in the street, school, market and even wider family, we must attempt to lessen the risks by being very close to them and through clear dialogue with them.

"It is natural for the father to go out with his family on an outside excursion or to partake in a pastime together. However, have you tried selecting only one child from your children to go out with him and have some food by yourselves without their being any theme for this feast other than taking an excursion or partaking in something enjoyable together? The minutes spent will then be precious and unforgettable.

"The illusion of Tarbiyah" ... On some occasions the relationship between the student and the educator turns into a relationship of friendship which is directly and indirectly devoid of direction. That is because the notion linked to the student accepting the educator and forming a solid relationship with him could lead to the formation of strong relationships albeit ones which do not yield benefit.

“The complete picture and extensive preparation” ... The educator needs to see the student from a distance as he will then be more capable of seeing his complete picture ... That is as daily interactions between the educator and student could divert the relationship from its required path, and we may discover later that we have not accomplished except a small amount in terms of instilling scattered manners and behavioural attitudes in the students, without having laid out for them a path or helping them in respect to shaping a life.

“When parents have children with special needs, that necessitates that the members of the household provide extra care and attention to them. However, that should not be accompanied by exaggerated pity that continuously makes them feel their weakness or deficiency. It should rather be done by simplifying, closeness, and natural interaction with them.

“The unmarried, divorced, or widowed woman is not more deficient than other women, requiring us to regard them with overburdening pity which only increases their suffering! They are rather women who have been subjected to particular circumstances which have put them in such a situation, whilst they may be more complete, cleverer, and beautiful than others.

“The father sitting with each of his children individually strengthens his relationship with them and makes him more knowledgeable about their different personalities and pressing needs in relation to education and giving direction.

Part Two

Thoreau said: "For every thousand hacking at the leaves of the tree, there's one striking at the root".

Developing the Practical Aspects

"Beware not to just transform the student into a depository for fuel alone: Rather, provide him with the vehicle to make use of this fuel through practical programs which set him into motion.

"The task of the teacher is to teach people that which is good. As for the educator (Murabbiy), then his task is to make them translate that goodness into the sensed reality.

"Be as diligent as possible to generate a kind of balance between the theoretical growth and the practical growth of the student, just as the car driver is very diligent to achieve balance in the wheels of his car.

"You will not be able to attain success in influencing the student unless it is through practical domains which you or the reality introduce him to. Your neglect to develop the practical aspect may take you by surprise at the time of crises, where you find that you constructed a great pyramid but one which was made from paper!

"Whenever you provide the student with theoretical direction, try to link it to a practical proposition for its application. Your continual effort to accomplish that could lead you to abandon much of your theoretical presentation which you will never find any practical implementation for in the reality.

"One, two, three ... ten ... one hundred ... The father asked his son whilst walking with him to the Masjid (mosque) to count his steps. Then after finishing the walk, he informs him that he has attained rewardable good deeds corresponding to the number of these steps, indeed many times greater than that! In this way he has presented to him an excellent practical lesson, firstly, in relation to the generosity and favour of Allah, and secondly, in relation to the virtue of going to the Masjid.

"We pay attention to encouraging our children to perform the Salah (prayer), but do we pursue them in respect to the manner of how to perform this prayer? And are they performing it as Allah wants it to be performed? That is where they perceive that they are engaged in the most important pillar and that they are standing before Allah, the Most Mighty and Majestic.

"One of the most important matters to build in the minds of our children is to make them accustomed to the love of reading. Included among the matters which can assist in realising that are: The presence of a small private library for them and a small monthly allocation of money specified for the purchasing of stories which they choose themselves.

"Training the child upon order helps him in the future to be able to manage his life successfully. From that which helps t`o develop that in him is: Specifying a designated time for everything, like watching television, sleeping, eating, studying, making family visits and playing.

"Ibn Taymiyah taught us an important educational principle in relation to providing a beneficial alternative, when he said: "People (or their inner selves) do not leave something unless it is for something (else). That is because the people (or their inner selves) have been created to do and not to leave".

“The successful educator is the one who utilises events and calamities which the Ummah (Islamic nation) passes through to strengthen and instil some concepts and values. Like for example: Cooperation, generosity, feelings of belonging to one single Deen (religion) and to plant high-minded aims within them.

“What is the value of good scientific research leading to an invention or discovery that realises a benefit for the people, if that research remains confined to the mind of the scholar or to the papers of his research, without being applied in real life?!

“I believe that you do not disagree that the logic of scientific knowledge belonging solely to scientific knowledge, and research solely to research, is an unacceptable and unbeneficial logic, which is more fitting for secluded philosophers than inviters and educators.

“It is important to comprehend well that the role of practical aspects is not only to compliment the theoretical aspects, but rather it is also to consolidate and strengthen them.

“The teacher, Khatib (orator), exhorter, cassette tape, book and others, perform the function of theoretical offloading, whilst you could almost be alone in respect to practising the practical unloading. However, when you lose this characteristic or quality and head in the direction of theoretical offloading alone, then you can choose to be anyone of those choices, as for the educator, then no!

“Investing in the educational raising of children is the real profitable investment ... If we spend our money in the way of education, acquiring qualifications, and to raise the educational, intellectual, technological and academic capabilities of our children, we would then at that time have placed our money in its most appropriate place!

Developing Initiative

"I believe that you agree with me that acting by one thought or idea from the suggestions of others is more impactful in respect to developing initiative within any one of them than tens of words of praise and delight provided in response to their thoughts and suggestions.

"It is an impossible equation that you wish to achieve when you follow up on all acts and views of the one you are educating in order to add to them or subtract from them, and thereafter request him to show initiative and creativity!

"The manner that encourages the initiator to use his initiative, is your own manner when you celebrate his correctness and overlook his error, and not your manner when you dig for errors and turn a blind eye to what is correct!

"Praise the past without adding "But" or "If only", and at that time you will be from those who produce initiative and develop it.

"It is important to deal with the person upon the basis of his good intention and not his mistaken initiative. That is if his good intention and purpose are preponderant in your view.

"To attain initiative from those you are educating, plant concern in their hearts ... That is because the one who carries a concern does not wait for someone else to innovate paths and means for him to act as an outlet and expression for this concern.

“How can you wish for a person to undertake a particular initiative if you have blocked him from all paths to access the initiative, through explicit instructions or commands in the smallest details which do not permit for the spirit of individual deduction and creativity to take place in or upon these matters.

“It is difficult for me to imagine an educator who kills the spirit of initiative in those he is educating by continuously focusing upon the examination of his errors ... However, I unfortunately witness this a lot from those undertaking this very role, when the educator attempts to allude to the perfection and best form of what matters should be, whilst forgetting encouragement and motivation for what has been completed and happened in the past.

Decision Making

“Do not make your objective with the student the development of his ability to make decisions alone, but rather also to develop his ability to make correct decisions.

“Taking the decision on behalf of the student is a process that buries the personality. Beware of doing this and instead provide your opinion to him in respect to what you view to be correct and leave the decision to him.

“Some educators practise a form of intellectual intimidation which makes it hard for the student to take a decision or adopt an opinion contrary to that of the educator. The educator may regard this practise to reflect a commendable influence in respect to taking correct decisions!

“It is not important to only make the student take the correct decision, but rather it is important for us to teach him how to continuously make this decision and without other external influences, in the case where the correct decision disappears in their absence. It is like the saying: “Don’t give me a fish, but rather teach me how to fish”.

“When you wish to implant the ability to make and take decisions in the student, you must also implant the ability to bear the burden of this decision in the case of it being incorrect or even correct. Otherwise, the life of the student will turn into one of constant regrets.

“Implant Tawakkul (reliance upon Allah) in the heart of the one you are educating. That is because the ability to take decisions requires a level of Tawakkul which the student turns to in for that which he is unable to determine from the matters which are unseen and unknowable to humans.

“Developing decision-making does not mean cancelling consultation. Rather, it is one of the factors for its success. However, do not make the student revolve in a large circle of consultations, which splinters the individual instead of guiding him.

“Strengthen (the concept and practise of) consultation within the student, however, also strengthen alongside it that the decision in the end is his and not that of the one he is consulting.

“You may be astonished when you know that when you demolish or cancel the personality of the student, intentionally or unintentionally, that you have not only shared in killing the capability to make decisions within his personality, but you have also participated in making him make bad or weak decisions, as not deciding is equivalent to making the bad or weak decision.

“Don’t pick up the red pen and proceed to mark all positions and decisions of the student as being correct or incorrect. By doing that you are committing an error greater than his error in respect to some of his decisions. That is because he, in truth, views that your red pen is erasing his mind and personality, and not his opinions and decisions.

Spiritual Transparency

"A practical experimental suggestion to entice children to read the Quran and to memorise it: Is for the child to record the section that he or she wants to memorise and then listen to it. In this manner, it will turn into a source of real enjoyment for the child, helping him to have interest in the Book of his or her Lord.

"The love of Allah is the greatest matter that the educator can implant within the one he is educating. A suggestion is for the educator to focus every week upon implanting one single attribute *(Sifah)* from His attributes *(Sifaat)*, Glorified be He, the Most High, utilising various and numerous ways to accomplish that.

"From the most beautiful concepts that we should implant within those we are educating is: "The yearning to meet Allah". That is because the one who yearns for Allah, Allah loves and protects. That is achieved by mentioning Him, praying to Him, speaking about Him, and reading His speech often.

"It may be that many can guide you to numerous aspects and many means to develop the worshipping aspect in others, however, remember that you personally and by your example will remain the greatest and most powerful means among all those means.

"The father asked his teenage son: "How long can you delay reading a text message sent to you by one of your closest friends?" The son answers: "I read it immediately". The father then asked: "And when was the last time that you read the message sent to you by your Lord to you: Al-Qur'an? The son answered sadly: "Last Ramadan!" So, the educating father said: "Whoever loves someone, loves everything that comes from him, whether it is speech, a command, or forbiddance".

"A simple question and before learning more methods of education: When was the last time that you raised your hands to Allah only for the sake of making a long and sincere supplication for your children? The Messenger of Allah ﷺ said: "**There are three supplications that are not rejected: The supplication of the father, the supplication of the oppressed (or wronged) and the supplication of the traveller**" Sahih (Authentic narration).

"Beware of igniting the fuse of Iman (belief) in the student without protecting it from going out within the glass of knowledge, education and comprehension. Also, beware of being in possession of that glass bottle of light without being in possession of the light itself.

"Attach the student to paradise and hellfire and make this fresh and vivid in his mind. That is because just as the self requires near term objectives, it will remain in the greatest need of paying consideration to that final goal which all those interim goals fall into.

""*Give us comfort with the Salah (prayer) O Bilal*" ... Raising the children upon the love of prayer so that it transforms from being a heavy burden that we pursue them upon to being a source of pleasure and enjoyment that they look forward to performing. There are numerous means to accomplish that, including: To continuously remind them of the wisdom of the Salah and not just its ruling.

"It is not that spiritual isolation that you need to implant within the one being educated, but rather it is that social spirituality that feeds and nurtures him instead of isolating him.

"When you think that you have completed the means of spiritual development of the one before you just because you have undertaken the greatest possible number of educational means which fall within this category, then you have fallen into a significant level of error ... Supplicate to Allah for Him to open the heart of your companion and remember that the exhaustion of sensed means does not mean the inevitable accomplishment of the results.

"The true primary factor that influences the student is what he sees from your conduct with him and not what he hears from the direction and instruction you provide to him.

"It should never be absent from your mind that every intellectual, knowledge-based (scientific) or invitational building not built upon a grounding of solid Iman (belief) is susceptible to collapse at any moment. Indeed, the higher the building gets without the presence of the foundation, the more terrible the fall and collapse will be.

"On many occasions the sick person is given an injection in other than the direct place of the pain. That is because it will travel in his blood to the intended place. Remember that, because perhaps you can treat a weakness in worship by an effective and indirect practical injection, like maintaining a good relationship, being a model example, leaving aside arguments and drawing focus upon the paths followed by righteous examples.

"It may be that you realise with me the seriousness or danger of neglecting the aspect of Iman (belief), when you know that everything you provide the student with in terms of knowledge, skills and capabilities, could turn against your goals if he loses his Iman based foundation from which he sets off from, and then only utilises what you have provided to him to accomplish his personal goals ... In such a case you would have in reality raised an enemy to you and your principles without even realising!

"It is nice to make to make our encouragement and rewarding of our children not based on giving money or gifts alone but also by way of supplication. So, we would say to them: "If you do such and such, we will supplicate for you". In this way, they will be raised upon the importance of the supplication in general and the supplication of the parents in particular.

"When we implant Iman well within our children, that will reflect positively in their kindness, good conduct and truthfulness with us and the people in general.

Dealing with Teenagers

“The teenage stage extends approximately between the ages of 12 and 18. It is a very significant stage in which new convictions are formed within the teenager. During it he attempts to establish himself and even if means going outside of the desired will of his family. It is very important for our motto during this stage to be: “Direction and not confrontation”.

“When our children reach the teenage stage dialogue and discussion must be the way to reach an understanding with them. That is as many teenagers complain that the role of the fathers and mothers is confined to giving them lectures and reprimands. In most cases, they are firstly repeated lectures, and secondly, the children don’t listen to them.

“The worst matter that can lead to the deviation of teenagers is the lack of closeness between them and their parents. They build their world, friends and interests in isolation to their families whilst the advice of their family holds no value to them. That is because the channel of communication between them has been cut. Therefore, if we want their ears to listen to us, we must first take possession of their hearts.

“Dr Abdul Karim Bakar said: “When children reach the age of a teenager, the practise of many children avoiding saying the truth becomes a clear matter. As such, if you are confronted by a solidly worked or tight story, make double sure before believing it. That is because the innocence of childhood has passed”.

“Even if the relationship of parents with their children is good, the influence of friends during the teenage stage is nevertheless greater than the influence of the parents. This demands from us to take care to surround our children with a distinguished circle of friends.

“During the teenager age parents are overcome by the feeling that everything they implanted in their children during their childhood has come to nothing and has had no impact! The reality, however, is that the bad characteristics have become apparent, like stubbornness, disorder, lack of respect and weak religious practise, whilst the good characteristics have taken a backseat until their impact appears and manifests later, by His permission تعالى.

“Are we truly close to our teenage children or does our relationship with them not go beyond the outer crust of their lives? That is whilst they live a complete life full of secrets and particularities which one day we may be unpleasantly surprised by!

“When our children approach the age of maturity, we need to deal with them like friends and speak clearly with them about the issues related to reaching the age of maturity and how to face them. This is especially important with girls. We must make completely sure of the quality of their particular environments, friends and school, lessen the number of commands, discuss with them and convince them, make them feel that they have really become adults and overlook their small mistakes.

“It is important that we do not to kill ambition of our children by going over the top in providing them with everything like a car and money etc. Rather, our children must feel that there are great efforts that they must undertake. That is because a life of comfort and luxury can destroy the serious raising process and destroy alongside that individual will and ambition.

“The friend has one of the biggest influences over the behaviour of a person whether he is old or young. Sometimes we don’t scrutinise the friends of our children because they are the children of their uncles and relations. It used to be said in the past: “Tell me who you keep company with, (then) I will tell you who you are”.

“Everything that we implant within our children by way of education and giving direction, runs the risk of being shaken apart if we do not also provide a particular environment of good friends and companions for them.

“All people take care of their children, however, few of them undertake their Tarbiyah (educational and character raising). That is because there is a major difference between Tarbiyah and caretaking. Tarbiyah means that we change the conduct of children and develop their personalities bit by bit. That is whilst caretaking is restricted to providing the main needs of the children, in terms of food, drink, clothing and shelter.

“The Prophet ﷺ said: “***A father gives his child no gift better than good manners***” (Narrated by Ahmad). Comment: All the amazing things that we provide to our children in terms of education, money, skills and other things, lose their quality of excellence and could transform into tools of corruption, if our children lose good manners and their morals are incomplete.

“Mothers should not let embarrassment or feelings of shame prevent them from teaching their daughters a lot of what she should know about her personal issues at the time of reaching the age of maturity. That is because the mother represents the safest path for delivering such beneficial information to her daughter.

Cultivating Drive and Ambition

"Cleverness is not what realises a dazzling future for our children: Rather, it is drive and industriousness (by the permission of Allah Ψ. That is because those who are industrious are capable of transforming their points of weakness into strengths, whilst inactiveness and laziness are the graveyard in which some clever people bury their intellects!

"Some young men and women possess great intelligence; however, they do not accomplish any success or distinction in their lives. In most cases, the reason is a problem related to industriousness, drive, clarity of objectives, or patience to develop the self and condition it.

"Mustafa Sadiq Ar-Raafi'iy said: "If you did not add anything to the Dunyaa (life of this world), then you were superfluous to it". We can change this statement into a question which cultivates positivity in the one being educated, by asking: "What is the additional thing which will increase your presence in your school, place of work, country or among your relatives and friends?

"Always try and make others believe in your idea before they carry it out. You will then notice the difference.

"A small box in which our children place a part of their daily allowances for their brothers in dire need, will implant within them the meaning of brotherhood and the spirit of generosity and giving.

"Compelling the student to carry out something which runs contrary to his personal interests or concerns, like compelling the child to drink medicine or to consume some kind of nutrition, may appear to be beneficial at first glance, but can quickly escape him due to your mere absence away from him!

"The example of the educator who was incapable of moving the belief in the goal into the orbit of the one he is working with, is like the train driver who wants to propel the train forward but without fuel!

"The real implementation of any thought begins from the mind and then after that the limbs respond to translate the convictions to apply them to real life.

"When you succeed in cultivating the desired drive and ambition within those you are educating, you will see from them that which you have sometimes not seen from yourself.

"Included among the most important matters that you should implant in those you are educating are: 1. The clarity of the objective and 2. The strong will. That is because the person without an objective is a lost person, whilst the objective without the will only amounts to hypothetical speech.

"Be completely confident that you will never be able to plant within the student a plant that you did not cultivate in your ground. That is because the drive is a feeling that is conveyed before it is meanings or concepts which are taught.

"Try to pass the stage of convincing the student with that which you want, to move to the stage of inflaming and igniting the fuse within these convictions for them to be launched into real life. This represents the important difference between the cold "intellectual" conviction and the ablaze "inner emotional" drive.

"Do not complain a lot about the shallowness of the interests or concerns of the one you are educating. Instead, generate for him serious concerns which are appropriate for his capabilities, then be sure that he will correct by himself all the previous unproductive concerns or interests.

"Cultivating the concern resembles what the process of a new birth for the student would be like, where he exits from his own world to enter a new life of the worlds of others and their concerns.

"The educator must make those around him live the reality that his Ummah (Islamic nation) lives. That is because events teach that which words cannot, and the passing comment upon a real-life event can have a far-reaching impact in respect to cultivating excellent qualities within those being educated.

"Parents supplicating for stricken and afflicted Muslims in front of their children and directing them towards that, implants within our children the meaning of brotherhood, elevates their concerns, and makes them feel their responsibility towards their Ummah (Islamic nation).

Emotional and Practical Sharing

"An hour of cooperation and joint action between you and the one you are educating has a far greater impact upon him than a torrential flow of instructions and advice which is free of association and interaction.

"It is nice that the student feels that you share in his own concerns, but even nicer than that is that you help him practically to deal with them.

"When the educator is capable of undertaking practical services for the student but then suffices with emotional and spoken sharing alone, then this sharing could be flipped from its positive form to its complete opposite.

"For certain, you don't possess a magic lamp like Aladdin to overcome all the student's difficulties, however, the student's feeling that had you possessed such a lantern, he would have been the first that you would have thought of, is sufficient for him to compensate for many of the on-the-ground actions towards him.

"Take great care that the power of your impact in the student stems from the power of your reality and your concerns but remember that this reality, however good it is, loses its shine when the student does not share in it. That is because people set into motion for themselves before they do so for others.

"Accomplishing the emotional and practical sharing with others is much easier than we think. It could be accomplished by a contact or communication outside the scope of shared concerns or by a question that is extra to what all the people ask him. It can be any simple and nontaxing act that you undertake every day.

“Others cannot accept you just because you have assisted them in some of their crises if you remain distant to them. They seek what is both greater and easier than that. They seek that you live their crises alongside them, even if you are unable to provide them with anything during that time!

“A single tear that comes from your eye in your interaction with the student due to a situation he is facing, is more impactful in his heart than if you were to give him $1000. That is because the tear comes from your eye, whilst the dollars come from your pocket. Having said that, how great would it be if both were combined!

“Be completely assured that positive feelings are not something manufactured, but are rather a reflection of a sincere concern the effects of which appear necessarily.

“He said to him: “This is my problem, so, are you able to help me out with such and such an amount?” The one being asked then lowered his head towards the ground saying with a weak voice that he could not help. Then early in the next morning he surprised him saying: “I saw in my dreams that I gave you the exact amount that you asked for!” At this point he answered him saying: “This dream is sufficient for me as you have truly given me that which is more precious than the money”.

“Open a special file in your heart for the student in which you pursue all his newly occurring realities and needs and treat this file with concern and secrecy. This will motivate the student to have greater trust, openness and interaction in respect to what you propose to him in terms of solutions and thoughts.

Dealing with Children

﴿يَٰٓأَيُّهَا ٱلَّذِينَ ءَامَنُواْ لَا تَخُونُواْ ٱللَّهَ وَٱلرَّسُولَ وَتَخُونُوٓاْ أَمَٰنَٰتِكُمْ وَأَنتُمْ تَعْلَمُونَ ٢٧﴾

«O you who have believed, do not betray Allah and the Messenger or betray your trusts while you know [the consequence]» *[Al-Anfal: 27]*

"Dealing with the children upon the basis that they are an Amanah (trust) increases our concern to educationally raise and direct them, and to expend all our possible efforts to protect them, until we meet Allah.

"When we purchase an electronic device, we read the manual that came with it to attain the most benefit from it and to not make mistakes when using it. Why then do we not do the same thing when Allah has provided us with children, in the case where we make an effort to read books related to raising and education (Tarbiyah) instead of relying upon personal experiences, the mistake in which may not be discovered until it is too late?

"Playing is a requirement ... The one who reflects upon the Prophetic Seerah (biographical life) can clearly observe that the Prophet ﷺ used to be forbearing and lenient in respect to some of what the children did when playing. Upon this basis, we must understand that play is an important need, even if it leads to the loss or relaxation of some of the forms of discipline and order that adults expect from children.

"Our dealings with our children must not only be restricted to issuing commands and forbiddances and meeting their desires. Rather, it should be based on dialogue, discussion, and living with each other, and indeed, even consulting them ... This is from that which strengthens their personalities, develops their minds, and increases our closeness to them and our accurate knowledge of their characters.

"The keenness of some parents to develop their children makes the parent deal with them as if they are adults, and he may forget that they are children with a need to play, amuse, and enjoy themselves.

"One of the most common mistakes is shaking children when they are crying. That is in the case where studies undertaken in Germany have confirmed that more than 100 children in Germany suffer severe brain damage annually as a result of being shaken when crying!

"From among the significant and strange matters as well is what some research has established in respect to the ability of the children to understand the character and personalities of their parents being greater than the ability of their parents to understand the personalities of their children!

"Do not praise the child just for being, but rather praise him for his good qualities or characteristics. So, for example, say to him or her: You are amazing because you are well-mannered... (or) because you treat your parents kindly and well ... (or) because you performed the Fajr prayer ... And continue to praise the child's good behaviour until it becomes a permanent characteristic or attribute of theirs.

"Many mothers complain about the repeated crying of their children. They may then intentionally attempt to silence them by forcibly preventing or hitting them! This has a negative impact upon the child. The outward crying will transform into an internal fear and terror, impacting upon the child's confidence in his personality when he grows up.

"Sheikh Ibn Uthaymeen was asked: "What is the description of how to read sections of the Qur'an upon children?" He answered: "(For the parent) to put their palms together, recite, blow in them and then wipe over the child".

"The best way to develop the minds of our children is to address them as if they are adults whilst not forgetting that they are children. That is because addressing them as adults develops their minds whilst not forgetting that they are children gives us cause to overlook their mistakes.

""He (the Prophet ﷺ) used to love the optimistic speech (or outlook)" ... Raising our children upon being optimistic strengthens their drive and resolve, helps them to deal with others positively and assists them to set goals for themselves and strive to accomplish them.

"It is important to decrease the time which our children spend playing electronic games during the time they spend playing. That is as many psychological studies have established that it implants aggressiveness within children, due to the reliance upon being stimulated by hitting, killing and wars.

“The child at the age of five considers his father to be the complete model, just like the daughter does with her mother. Both expend a great effort to satisfy and please their parents by imitating them, which obliges the parents to be of a high level in terms of being an example and possessing awareness.

“It is beautiful what has been narrated from the biographical life of the Prophet Al-Mustafa ﷺ about how he used to specify some children with secrets, an act providing a powerful moral boost. So, why do we not, as a suggestion, make from our intention to buy something valuable in the house or to go out on a particular trip, a secret which we tell specifically to one of our children, in an alternate manner. We would then make them feel special and close to us, in addition to raising their confidence to carry responsibilities.

“Look at your child for a long time when sleeping and reflect upon the child’s points of excellence and weaknesses. Then address yourself saying: How can I demand a lot from my child despite their young age? How can I measure my child by the same measure dictated by my age and experience? And does this poor child deserve to be hit or shouted at and for me to rage against them in such a manner?

“The Messenger of Allah ﷺ was playful with a young boy whose little bird died, saying: “***O Abu ‘Umair, what did the Nughair (a kind of bird) do?***”. Comment: Providing a Kunya (a name with father “Abu” in it, like Abu Khalid or Abu Muhammad etc.) makes him sense his own personality and independence and generates in him the spirit of responsibility and sense of being a man (or adult).

"Sa'd bin Malik was a young boy whose father was martyred at the battle of Uhud. When Al-Mustafa, the Prophet ﷺ, returned from the battle he said to him: "***Are you Sa'd bin Malik***?" He replied: "Yes, may my father and mother be ransomed for you". He then said: "***May Allah reward you for your father***". Being concerned with the feelings of the young and treating them like adults elevates their level and prepares them for the hardships of life.

"And he ﷺ would line up Abdullah and Ubaidullah the sons of Al-'Abbas in a row and then say: ***"The one who races to me first will attain such and such". They would then race until they both reached him, and then he would kiss them and hug them.*** Comment: Planting competitiveness among the children increases their drive and ambition and brings out their talents.

"Satisfy your children emotionally, play with them, fill your mouth with water and spray them with it, stick out your tongue at them until they see its redness, and carry them upon your back as if you were a camel and take them around the room wherever they wish. If they climb upon your back while you are in prostration, then make the prostration longer for their sake. The Prophet ﷺ used to do all of this.

"A person taking care of his children is an excellent and required matter, whilst his taking care of the children of his neighbours and relatives is even more beautiful and excellent. As for his goodness and giving being extended to the children of the Muslims in general including the orphans and needy, then that will bring the best effect and blessing upon him and his children in the life of this world and the hereafter.

"Mu'adh and Mu'awwidh raced to the Messenger of Allah ﷺ at the end of the battle of Badr, each of them giving the glad tidings that he was the one who had killed Abu Jahl. Al-Mustafa ﷺ looked at both their swords and then pleased them both saying: "***Both of you killed him***" ... Comment: It is nice to ignite the spirit of competitiveness among our children, however, it is even nicer for us to praise everyone that took part in an act, even if the results of some are less than others.

"Telling stories are from the very beneficial ways to impact people in general and children in particular. And let us remember that Allah, Glorified be He the Most High, made a third of His Book consist of stories of the previous nations.

"The Messenger of Allah ﷺ used to greet the children, entrust them with a secret, let them sit in his meetings, attend his Masjid, joke with them, provide them with a Kunya (name with "Abu" in it) and play with them, whilst he never struck a child in his life.

"It is important that we discover early the points of strength and distinction of each of our children, whether that relates to the computer, reading, writing or other than that, so that we can develop these points within them and assist them to achieve distinction in them. One of the most important aspects of Al-Mustafa ﷺ in relation to Tarbiyah is that he knew how to develop the points of strength in those around him.

"Have you ever apologised to your child? If you want to strengthen the art of apology, gratitude, good manners and love in your children, then be the model example in respect to that.

Apologise if you made a mistake, thank them is they have done something nice and treat them with love and respect.

“The Messenger of Allah ﷺ used to seek protection for Al-Hasan and Al-Husain saying: “I seek protection for you in the Perfect Words of Allah from every devil and vermin, and from every envious blameworthy eye”. This is from that which protects the children from the (evil) eye (of envy).

“Not everything produced for children is suitable for them in terms of magazines and television or satellite channels, like Tintin, Mickey mouse, Mickey pocket magazine, Spacetoon and Police puzzles, which the Arab child receives just like the non-Arab child without any alteration in its content.

“Our children are like a fertile ground. If we plant healthy and good seeds in it, the plant will grow well and its fruit will become ripe. However, if we leave it, neglect it and become preoccupied away from it, others will plant upon it what they wish and the thorns that grow in it will come back to hurt us.

“It has been related from the Prophet ﷺ that he said: “The feistiness (or mischievousness) of the child in his childhood acts to increase his intelligence in his adulthood”. This means that if the child moves a lot and constantly plays, then that will increase his intelligence and skills when he becomes an adult.

“Every child must attain their right in respect to individual Tarbiyah (educational and behavioural raising). As such, the child needs to sit with his parents alone and go out and talk with them on an individual basis. That is because collective Tarbiyah could negate or cancel out each child's needs which differ from another's.

"At a time when the oldest son wins appreciation and respect and the youngest son receives affection and pampering, the middle son may end up deprived of all of that. This makes it necessary for us to provide each child from among our children their complete right in terms of caretaking and concern.

"Just as each one of our fingers has a specific print which differs from the other, then each of our children has their special needs which differ from the rest of their siblings. We have to discover these special qualities to invest and develop them in the appropriate manner.

"The child tries to test out everything that adults say to him. So, for example, when we say to the child, "Do not go close to the iron because it is hot", he will not believe it and will attempt to get close to it and touch it. After that, he will believe that it is hot, because it has practically burnt him.

The Model Example

"Being an example means that you represent what you believe and say, and not that you act that out. That is because one of the greatest matters that we must beware of is for the educator to transform into an actor.

"Just as you will be one of the most positive influences for the student through your good example, you will also be one of the most negative influences upon him through your bad example, regardless of your other good influences.

"If you are from those who always say what they don't do, then you will constantly see in the one you are addressing that which you did not say!

"Beware of being from those who scold themselves. That is because only the one whose speech does not conform to his actions ends up scolding himself!

"Address the one you are educating by your actions before you address him with your speech. That is because "Words are mere bubbles of water, but deeds are drops of gold".

"The educator needs to constantly revise himself to complete the aspects of deficiency within him. The role of the educator cannot be to develop others whilst he forgets to develop himself:

﴿۞أَتَأۡمُرُونَ ٱلنَّاسَ بِٱلۡبِرِّ وَتَنسَوۡنَ أَنفُسَكُمۡ وَأَنتُمۡ تَتۡلُونَ ٱلۡكِتَٰبَۚ أَفَلَا تَعۡقِلُونَ٤٤﴾

«Do you order righteousness of the people and forget yourselves while you recite the Scripture? Then will you not reason?» [Al-Baqara: 44]

"During the times of distress, tests, and examinations, the student does not remember what he heard from you. Rather, he remembers what he saw from you.

"The profession of Tarbiyah does not suit those who believe that addressing the student by words and statements is sufficient, whilst forgetting that the one who plants words does not reap except illusions.

"Your negative influence upon the one being educated increases as you increase your advice and direction to him, but, of course, that is only true after you have generated a great gap between what you say and what you do.

"It is not possible for a man who is shy or embarrassed of his higher principles to be a successful educator or a leader of men.

"There is no problem or issue for the educator to display some of his good actions for them to be an example to be followed. That is because people are influenced by seeing the conduct more than by hearing of it. Displaying good acts with the intention of teaching and raising others is also a good action in itself.

"Improve your image as much as you are able, however beware of displaying another image or form which is not your true image or form. That is because you will not be able to continue upon that. Rather, you are required to improve and develop your own true image and not to act out or demonstrate an image that does not even exist in origin!

“The impact of the real educator is not attained from his position as a teacher, father or guide. Rather, it comes from his sincere concern and his true love for the one he is making effort to have an impact upon. That is because people are very resistant to those who are elevated and in a domineering position over them, whilst they are very easy and pliant with those who respect them and show them appreciation.

“The people are in great need of upright examples whose integrity they sense, who rise above all that is dishonourable and whose impact they see in the reality by their actions more than their speech. It is like Ibn ul-Jawziy said: “The guide by action guides more than the guide by speech”. Regardless of how beautiful our guidance and direction are, people will never respond positively to us until our actions are also beautiful.

“Many fathers and mothers complain of the unyielding attitudes and obstinacy of their children. However, when investigating the causes, we discover that the unyielding attitudes of the parents themselves is one of the most significant causes of that.

“Al-Hafizh Al-‘Iraqiy mentioned that the number of Sahabah (companions of the Prophet ﷺ) named Abdullah totalled approximately three hundred. This reflects a beautiful emulation from which its blessing is hoped for the child. That is because the name has its impact upon the one who bears it, as was mentioned by Sheikh ul-Islam (Ibn Taymiyah) and others from the people of knowledge.

“Our positive conduct in our treatment of servants has the most far-reaching impact in respect to elevating the manners and moral characteristics of our children who are carefully watching that. It then reflects positively upon their conduct with the rest of the people.

"The Messenger of Allah ﷺ said: "***Pray as you see me pray***" and he said: "***Take from me your rituals (i.e. in the Hajj)***". That is whilst Aa'ishah (may Allah be pleased with her) described him saying: "***His Khuluq (character) was the Qur'an***". The best, quickest and most powerful way to impact the students is for the good example to be present before them

"A man was sitting with the Prophet ﷺ. His son then approached and so he kissed him and then sat him in his room. Then a daughter of his came but he did not kiss her. So, the Messenger of Allah ﷺ said to him: "***Do you not treat them equally***?!" Justice and fairness among children are not restricted to the material things, but rather it extends to the non-material and emotional matters.

"It is true that our children are in need of Tarbiyah (an educational and behavioural raising) ... However, our need for that is greater! That is because many of the children's behaviours which we complain about are nothing but an accurate mirror of our own moral and manner-based characteristics. Why do we get angry when our young children repeat the same mistake on numerous occasions, whilst we have been falling into the same mistake for tens of years!

"The Prophet ﷺ said: "One of you sees the speck in his brother's eye, whilst he forgets the (tree) trunk in his own eye". Comment: If we can be versatile in creating excuses and justifications for our own errors, then why can't we also be so with the errors and lapses of others?! The successful educator cannot be someone who hunts for errors.

"We cannot change others if we have not succeeded in changing ourselves. And we will never be the best and most suited to giving guidance and education only because we say the best speech. Rather, it will be because we do the best action.

"It is not appropriate to make our children exactly like us. That is because we are not the best and the successful educator is the one who benefits the student from his points of strength without transferring to him his points of weakness.

"We must admit that we could be weak in many of the areas which those we are addressing require. This means that we should not make ourselves the only teacher and guide. That is because when we make ourselves the final and ultimate reference point, we will never be able to produce except those who are weaker than us.

"If the student was an exercise book in which you wrote all of your points of guidance, then it would be your right to revise this exercise book to see the impact of what you had written. That is so that you do not become surprised after a long period of time by discovering that you have been writing with a pen that has no ink, due to the pen being bad or the ink being dry?!

"The main qualities of the educator include "Patience and forbearance". That is because the human is not a machine where we press its buttons and it responds immediately. Rather, the human is a being with a changeable temperament and his ability to change his deep-rooted character is not an easy matter.

"Be sure that you will never be able to cultivate in the ground of the student a plant that you did not cultivate in your own ground. That is because the major concerns represent feelings that are transmitted before they are concepts which are taught.

"The characteristics of our children are no more than an accurate mirror of our own characteristics. Activeness or laziness, truthfulness or dishonesty, being well mannered or being bad mannered. These are characteristics which we cultivate in our personalities and then they sprout within the conduct of our children.

"Included among the very beneficial styles to educate and raise our children to be be kind to us, is for the husband to respect his wife and for the wife to respect her husband. That is because the child stringently imitates what he sees from his parents.

"Children strongly imitate what they witness. The treatment that they witness from their parents towards their grandparents reflects the manner of how they will treat their parents when they become adults. Therefore, the one who wants to know whether his children will treat him well and with kindness, should examine the level of kindness and good treatment he provided to his parents, as the recompense corresponds in kind to the act.

"We must educate and raise our children upon respecting those in weaker positions, like the servant, driver, worker and child. We will not be able to raise them upon that unless we are their model and example. Our concern with that will reflect positively upon their treatment of all people, by Allah's permission.

"The Prophet ﷺ housed the poor Sahabah, who were known as Ahl us-Suffah, behind his house and not in remote isolated areas. He would feed them from his own food and clothe them from the garments which were available to him. Comment: Our good treatment towards those who serve us represents an important educational message for our children which will reflect upon their conduct and manners with all people.

"The educator should be concerned with presenting stories of model examples in all areas and fields from the past and present. That is because this style has a greater impact upon people than the impact of the educator's speech. It also represents a way for the educator to cover in his educating some of what he is missing in his own reality and conduct.

"Al-Aqqad said: "You do not need to raise your voice when you are informing me that 1+1=2, however, you will need to raise your voice and make use of your cunning and wile to convince me that 1+1=3". The calmness of the educator and his dignified bearing is evidence of the truthfulness of his speech and it represents the way to convince the student.

""Everything has its levy (or charge or toil) and nothing is without cost". This is an important educational principle. That is because in the story of the believing wife Hajar and her baby Isma'eel, the water did not gush forth from under his feet until after her feet had become tired out from rushing back and forth seven laps whilst searching for water. This is the nature of human efforts in this life:

﴿لَقَدْ خَلَقْنَا ٱلْإِنسَٰنَ فِى كَبَدٍ ۝٤﴾

«We have certainly created man into hardship» *[Al-Balad: 4]*

"One of the greatest harms that afflicts the educator is that his goodwill is met by bad will or mistreatment, and his keen attention and concern are snubbed! However, if the person keeps at the forefront of his mind that Allah recompenses the goodwill and good treatment towards others with a goodness that is better than it, it will lessen the effect of the people's snubbing of him, and he will attain the greatest compensation. So, the one who has found Allah, what has he lost?! Whilst, the one who has lost Allah, what has he found?!

"Nuh (Noah) was afflicted with his son, Ibrahim with his father, Lut with his wife and Muhammad with his uncle, may the peace and blessings of Allah be upon them all, whilst none had a stronger desire and concern to guide their family members and relatives than them. In this way, the educator makes the greatest effort possible, however, he knows that the guidance of hearts is something beyond his capabilities.

"Allah Ψ said:

﴿وَأْمُرْ أَهْلَكَ بِٱلصَّلَوٰةِ وَٱصْطَبِرْ عَلَيْهَا ۖ﴾

«And enjoin prayer upon your family [and people] and be steadfast therein.» *[Ta-ha: 132]*

Here, Allah made a connection between the statement of the father or the mother commanding the performance of the Salah (prayer) and their steadfastness upon its performance. This is an indication of the importance of the example and role model in relation to the children responding positively to their parents.

““Your smile towards the face of your brother is a Sadaqah (a rewardable act of charity)”. However, the smile provided to your children represents a Sadaqah, connection, affection, and education. It is unfortunate that some fathers and mothers deprive their children of their smiles whilst resorting to constant yelling, reproaching, and blaming.

“Be sure to change the conduct of others through your own conduct and not through your speech. In testing situations, the student does not remember what he heard from you, but rather what he saw from you.

“When we teach our children to say some well-mannered expressions with their siblings inside the house, like “please”, “if you don’t mind”, and “thank you”, then they will get used to saying them outside of the house as well, and it will become a part of their personalities.

““The Prophet ﷺ forbade insulting the wind and animals”. Comment: When the person becomes accustomed to being decent and respectful in speech when it comes to animals and inanimate objects, then by greater reason, he will conduct himself in a similar manner with all people.

“Sometimes you can do everything that should lead to positively impacting others, and yet you do not accomplish what you desire! This calls for us to have reliance upon the Tawfeeq (success and attainment) of Allah, the Mighty and Majestic, and not upon our own abilities to accomplish the objectives. It also prompts us to anticipate our reward in the hereafter when our efforts in the life of this world do not achieve their results:

﴿إِنۡ أَجۡرِيَ إِلَّا عَلَى ٱللَّهِ﴾

«My reward is only from Allah» *[Yunus: 72]*

"The desire to appear with the appearance of the model example makes some give pretence to perfection whilst concealing their weaknesses. In most cases, this leads to an opposite result, as the educator will appear like a failing actor and not an educator and model example.

""Start with yourself" ... It is not acceptable for an educator in an age which is mainly characterised by recency and speed to be slow in developing himself as much as he can. Otherwise, the time will pass him by regardless of his wishes. The main message of the educator with his students and children cannot possibly be for them to develop in a variety of fields and to change their circumstances to what is better, whilst he remains in a stagnated state without making any progression.

Part Three

Thoreau said: “For every thousand hacking at the leaves of the tree, there’s one striking at the root”.

Inner Stability

"It is not enough to present knowledge and good conduct to the student. It is necessary to shape his personality by making it stable internally and far removed from the acute and unexpected anomalies, over-emotional reactions, and complicated psychological twists.

"You cannot address the minds of people when their stomachs are empty. So, what about the situation when their hearts are wandering and unsettled?!

"Included among the main actions that you can do to instil inner stability is to provoke the student with adult concerns and remove him from the narrow world that he lives in. If, however, you were to attempt to treat every small personal concern of his, you would perhaps be forced to forgo your own larger concerns?

"Take extra care to develop the self-confidence of the student as it is an important factor for the realisation of inner stability. If you are unable, then the least you can do is increase the student's confidence in you. That is because when people cannot find within their own personalities that which they can rely upon, they look to those around them to find within them that which they cannot find within themselves.

"The mental and emotional disposition of the student is like a vessel or bottle. If it was to break or was unable to stabilise, then everything you place inside it and educate it upon in terms of your educational and invitational goals would not settle and become stable.

“Nothing irritates the student like not being able to identify the personality of the one undertaking his direction and educational raising. In such a circumstance, he would expect anything from him regardless of how irregular it was, leading him to lose the sense of security. As such, the stability and balance of the educator is an important characteristic, and its positivity or negativity also reflects upon the stability of the student.

“If you can reach, amend, and adjust the mental and emotional disposition of the student, it will assist you to disperse your seeds upon the ground that you had cultivated previously. Don’t be misled by the apparent external gains of the student. That is because any apparent external changes not based upon internal inner changes are prone to collapse at any time.

“Make sure of the well-being of the vessel”: Emotional and mental stability are among several qualities that are important to be present within the student’s personality. That is because the personality that suffers from a weakness in its emotional and mental stability is a vessel that is not suited to be filled with responsibilities and concerns.

“From among the fruits of mental and emotional stability: The emotionally and mentally unstable person is not backward or deficient! He may well be intelligent and talented, but is an unbalanced person in his conduct and thinking. That is because the balance in conduct and calmness of mind are from the greatest fruits and indications of mental and emotional stability.

“Building the mind and the emotional state” ... Building the composed mind accompanied by nourishing the balanced emotional state are from the matters which lead to a balanced mental and emotional personality. Exaggeration, intensity and extremeness in thinking, and severe hesitancy and emotional drowning, are all matters which must be under the observation of the educator and his treatment.

"The crippled building" ... On some occasions the educator could partake, albeit with a good intention, in weakening the student's level of emotional and mental stability. That is when his building of him is crippled i.e. not complete or comprehensive. That is where he neglects important and impactful matters related to his personality, like the consolidation of his material situation, for example, or reconciling his social position, like marriage for example, and what resembles such matters.

"There is a clear contradiction between our constant complaints about the deviations of the male and female youth around us, and between the large dowries and many burdens and obstacles we place before them in the way of marriage, which then leads to not facilitating the paths of chastity for them!

"The eagerness of some parents to keep their children away from trouble, makes them move in the direction of preoccupying them with electronic devices, such as smartphones and tablets. This then generates a kind of addiction which can lead to introverted and antisocial children, who have a lower social intelligence, as has been established by many studies.

Solving Problems

"Before anything, you must first clearly identify the problem. That will help you, after that, to analyse and understand the problems, in order to put down successful and practical solutions for them. Their implementation and evaluation will take place when you are convinced of their usefulness.

"You would be in an excellent position if you are not waiting for problems to arise to the surface in order to solve them, but rather pluck out their roots before they appear and become aggravated. The wise person is not the one who is good at putting out fires after they have been set alight. Rather, he is the one who puts the safety measures in place which prevent the fire from starting in the first place.

"Remember, that the first quality from the qualities that deal with solving problems is for the educator to be a good listener. Indeed, many problems of people come to an end by merely finding someone to listen to everything they are saying and to understand what they want!

"Beware of confronting problems with preconceived and pre-packaged solutions. You will lose your point of reference in respect to solving problems when others can already tell what you are going to say to them when they present their problems to you.

"Think with freedom and with no restrictions: This free thinking will grant you power, distinctiveness, and the ability to come up with the best solutions.

“Take as much care as possible to not generate any void or gap between the two pivots of the problem. Try to have a lot of open free speaking sessions. That is because the gaps that can occur between the two pivots of a problem are a main cause for the generation of incorrect thoughts, bad suppositions and far off improbable explanations and interpretations.

“Don’t be idealistic where you request others to remove themselves from the problem merely because you have convinced them of that. That is because convincing is not everything ... Rather, provide others with the opportunity through time for your solutions to be consolidated or for the brevity of the problem to be calmed down within them. Remember, that the Prophet Al-Mustafa ﷺ permitted three days for those who have argued from the time of separation to make amends

“Separating the problem from the one who has it could lead to impractical or unsuccessful solutions, just as setting off from the premise of the person’s background leads you to pass judgement upon the one who has the problem and not the problem itself.

Taking on Responsibility

"It is important to teach children to take on responsibility. Included in that is entrusting them with some actions. The mother can ask herself: "What are the things which I am always doing but my child could do by his or herself if I wasn't to do them?" She then proceeds to leave these actions in a gradual manner.

"Before educating the student to take on responsibility, convince him first that it is a responsibility. That is as actions not based on a good level of conviction are not kept up for long.

"Beware of throwing the student into the sea with his hands tied and thereafter ask him not to drown ... Requesting the student to take on a particular responsibility should be in harmony with his capabilities; those capabilities which you are supposed to be one of the most significant participants in respect to bringing into being.

"How can the student take on responsibility if he has not been provided with the opportunity to fail? Yes, your concern upon the success of the student must not make you deprive him of the opportunity to fail ... Let the student undertake some responsibilities by himself, even if it is in an imperfect manner, and then you shall see the fruits.

"There are times when the son needs time to think before acting, so do not volunteer to solve his problems in place of him. Leave him to think so that he can bring solutions by himself, whilst at the same time not making yourself distant from him.

“You will never be able to instil the spirit of responsibility in the student by merely delivering a few words to his ears. Rather, it will only happen when you practically entrust him with some responsibilities which correspond to his capabilities.

“Remember that the student’s feeling of belonging to something represents the path towards sacrificing for it. Strengthen within the student the spirit of belonging to that which you want him to accomplish before everything else.

“You will never be able to increase the student’s spirit of taking on responsibility by constantly pointing out to him that he is falling short in his performance of this or that responsibility. Rather, you will only accomplish it by reaffirming his capability to undertake and assume it.

“Take care to increase the practical unloading as you increase the theoretical loading. That is because making the student feel that there are a huge number of responsibilities entrusted to him, whilst not providing the practical mechanisms to release this feeling, afflicts the student with the feelings of hopelessness, disaffection and incapability.

“Do not make the student drown in seas of responsibility which he does not know how to swim in. That is as the responsibility which the heart of the student should be filled with is his responsibility to undertake that which he is capable of and not that which he in not capable of.

“Before consolidating the positive spirit of responsibility remove the negative obstacles. The feeling of possessing a lack of means, weak confidence, incapability, the impediment of fear, monotony, preoccupation with personal concerns and matters similar to these, represent a solid wall which must be demolished in order to reach through to the mental and emotional disposition of the student and make him feel responsibility.

“In the battle of Uhud, the Prophet ﷺ consulted his companions in relation to where the battle should take place and he followed their opinion. That was followed by defeat but the Prophet Al-Mustafa ﷺ did not blame his companions with a single word” ... When we blame others for results related to matters which we consulted them in, then that indicates that we were not really looking for someone to consult, but rather for someone to blame for our mistakes (if things go wrong).

“Melinda the wife of Bill Gates, the richest man in the world said: “We take care to raise our children upon austerity and being moderate in spending” pointing to the fact that “The blessing may not continue indefinitely, just as it is important that even the rich feel the importance of working and eating from the fruits of their hard work!”.

Social Competency

"An important fact of education and raising is that: Children who have everything they want fulfilled for them are not happier than other children. Rather, fulfilling everything that our children want kills off ambition within them and makes them unqualified to deal with the challenges of life. As for their real happiness in relation to material things, then that is only realised when they expend a great effort to attain them.

"It is for certain that you don't want to produce a man who is isolated from his reality and a failure in social interaction, regardless of his position, whether it is as a father, citizen, relative or friend. We are not only referring to communication skills here but rather the skills to acclimatise, harmonise and interact as well. This is exactly what we mean when referring to social competency.

"Do not be excessive in respect to injecting the student with a needle harbouring criticism and resentment upon his society because it is a corrupt society. By doing that you will be building within him a mental and emotional barrier opposed to this society which includes those who are closest to him. You will then be passing a sentence upon him of social introversion followed by (a social) death.

"The Messenger of Allah ﷺ used to love his homeland of Makkah and he cried in sadness upon his departure from it when the disbelievers of Quraish drove him out. Consequently, the love of the homeland is not incompatible with the love of the Deen (religion). Raising our children upon the love of their homelands makes them elements which are not only beneficial and productive for them but also which repel bad from them.

"The Prophet ﷺ said: "A believer who mixes with people and endures their annoyance is better than the one who does not mix with them and does not endure their annoyance" ... Get our children accustomed to mixing with others increases their capabilities and preparedness, just as it helps us to acquire an accurate understanding of their personalities. Whilst on the other hand, instilling exaggerated fear in them based upon the argument of the badness of others, deprives them of all these benefits.

"When we seclude ourselves from the people because we feel that we are purer than them in heart or spirit, we would not have accomplished anything significant. True greatness is accomplished when we mix with those people whilst being contented with what we have of concepts and principles. Then we proceed to raise them to our level without descending to their level" ... This is a shade from the shades of social competence which Sayyid Qutb, may Allah's mercy be upon him, taught us.

"It is not enough to convince the student of the necessity of social interaction without providing him with the practical mechanisms to build that interaction. Direct him towards communication skills and practical or vocational skills that are common in his society.

“Instil within the student that people accept those whom they feel live the same lives as them and not those who are approaching them from a different planet.

“Young children attending the gatherings of their parents leads to them acquiring adult norms which develop their personalities. On the other hand, making them over scared of mixing with people leads them to being deprived of many life skills.

“Expand the scope of the student’s culture ... Here, I am not only referring to the culture of the Shar’iyah or that related to education. Rather, I also mean the social culture represented in examples, knowledge of places, routes and main public gathering places. It also means making them familiar with the reality of the people, their living, customs, relations, and what they are like.

“Reinforce the spirit of mercy in the heart of the student and not the spirit of dissatisfaction and resentment. Teach him that mercy does not mean overlooking the mistake of the wrongdoer, but rather to prevent him and rid him of it, followed by positive interaction with him.

“Prepare the student for a good material life ... That is because severe material deficiency makes the student feel some social deficiency. If he was secured from that, then perhaps he would not be secured from the view of others towards him. If he were, however, secured from both this and that, then perhaps the scope of his influence would remain limited due to his being preoccupied with his efforts to earn a living or by his lack of means, which takes him away from translating many of his convictions with those around him.

"To be balanced and successful in your educational raising in respect to preparing the student for a suitable level of social competency, then in addition to what you have undertaken in terms of refining his conduct and personality, it is necessary to educate him socially by making him aware of the skills of domestic dealings for when he becomes a father or husband. It is also necessary to provide him with consumer skills and indeed, even some essential vocational home skills!

"Do not build the student in the form of someone who is lagging behind his reality and society, based upon the pretext that he has a specialised Shar'iy interest alone. That is because at such a time he would never be capable of making progress with them.

"Taking into account the external influences" ... The educator must always bear in mind the influences surrounding the student and deal with them in an appropriate manner. These influences appear in family surroundings, amongst old friends, material status and the social environment. When the Prophet ﷺ used to educate his companions, he would bear in mind the environment and tribe of the one he was educating, and indeed, even his smaller direct family.

"Upside-down scales" ... From among the major errors that we can fall into when we do not consider the environment of the student and his background, is that we prepare him for an environment different to his. We could also take him to task for that which he would not be taken to task for within his society, as if we are setting for him upside-down scales!

“For sure, you did not understand from being asked to socially prepare the student that this includes giving him a lesson in cooking skills, or how to change a car tyre, or how to make purchases in the market? However, do you not agree with me that neglecting the student in these areas and isolating him from them through not introducing him to them, based on the reasoning that they will naturally come to him (in time) or that there are more important things to be taught, may well pose a problem for him in the future! In the past it was said: “Most disasters are the result of seemingly insignificant matters which you neglected!”

“The true reality of educational raising is that it is what prepares our children to successfully deal with themselves, their families and friends in the various aspects of life. It is not as most parents think in that Tarbiyah only means obedience and good manners alone!

How is the student protected from the effects of your Tarbiyah mistakes with him?

"Beware of preventing the student from seeing anything except through you. By doing that you would only be making him a blind follower and not an insightful leader.

"Remember that the student is not a piece of private furniture belonging to you. Widen the scope of his relationships and beware of practising a form of intellectual blocking which he will be the first to suffer from.

"The student must feel that the educator is a reference point for him, however, don't make yourself the scales through which the student must weigh all his statements and actions.

"On some occasions there is no problem to overlook some of your deductions which you believe to be correct ... Give yourself and others the opportunity to take in some air.

"Admitting the error, opening a dialogue, contenting the student and revision are equivalent to the curbs and brakes for your educational mistakes with the student and even if some time has passed by.

"When you go beyond the stage of the student respecting you to the stage of him exalting or glorifying you, then regardless of the emotional and mental dispositional negatives brought upon him, you would have set solid foundations for the acceptance of all your mistakes with him without scrutiny or checking.

“Before thinking about treating the effects of your errors with the student, take as much care as you can to not fall into error in the first place, through some means, the most significant of which can be to make more than one educator share in your pursuance of the student.

“Admitting the error is praiseworthy, however, when that is repeated a lot, it turns into a failing indicating your deficiency in relation to that which you repeat the error in and apologise for.

“Do not fill the ears, eyes and heart of the student with speech about your own personal affairs, in terms of what you usually or don’t usually do, what you like and dislike, how you drive your car, sleep, eat and drink etc. This will only reinforce in him that you don’t see anyone in existence apart from yourself. After that, how do you expect him to keep clear of your educational errors with him?!

Correcting the Errors

"Two people may correct the error of a particular person and yet he only accepts that from one of them and not the other. That is because one of them focuses upon the error, whilst the other focuses upon the person who has made the error!

"Regardless of how many the mistakes of the one you are educating may be, you must search for his good points and emphasise them. If you do not do that, then in his view you would have turned into a source of irritation and scolding instead of a source of education and guidance.

"Don't make the student go to pains in his attempt to clear himself from the error. Rather, undertake that yourself, and then you will find a heart that is open to you and to your teachings.

"Beware when correcting the student's error not to fall into another error, like using an inappropriate style, going over the top or not differentiating between the error and the one who made it etc. If you were to do that then he would forget his own mistake and only remember yours.

"Do not curse him, for verily he loves Allah and Messenger" ... The educator needs to reinforce his respect for others, even if he is punishing or rebuking them when the matter demands that. The need to receive respect is a persistent need of a person's personality and nature. An educator relying upon his authority among his students whilst not observing this need represents a dangerous risk that could put an end to the basis of the relationship between them.

"Your role is not to continuously point with your finger at the mistake. Rather, it is to extend your hand to the student to assist him to exit from the mistake. This reflects one of the important differences between the educator and the policeman.

"The proverbial wisdom states: "Not every fall is the end, because rainfall represents the best beginning" ... The astute educator is the one who makes a positive beginning from the error that others fall into to change their personalities towards what is better.

"We do not only wish for the people and ourselves to admit that we are only humans who can get things both right and wrong. That is because that conclusion is from the obvious matters of the ration and Deen! Rather, we actually want to retreat from our errors instead of going to lengths to justify or defend them.

"It is not the role of the educator to treat all aspects of deficiency in himself and others. We must accept the existence of a natural weakness which is difficult to treat. This does not however mean that we do not look for aspects of strength which through their development and strengthening could overcome those aspects of deficiency.

"People by their nature incline towards seeing the error before seeing what is right. That is whilst the successful educator needs to commend what is correct more than criticising what is incorrect, in order to instil inspiration and motivation. Ash-Shafi'iy said: "If I was correct 99% and was mistaken 1% (of the time), the people would leave (or forget) what I was correct in and openly announce that which I was incorrect about!".

“We must have the ability to discover the virtues of others and their positive points accompanied by developing them and commending them. The educator who does not see anything apart from errors is nothing more than a punisher who views the people as prisoners to their errors and consequently contributes to keeping these errors permanently in them.

“You can correct a certain error of the student, however by making him feel that you are developing that which is correct, or after having addressed something that is correct with him you can move on to correct something that is incorrect with him. In this way the warmth of this will remove the coldness of that. The Hadith stated: “What an excellent servant Abdullah is! If only he were to perform prayer during the night”.

“Before proceeding to correct an error of the student take care to treat the causes that have led to this error. That is because the wise educator does not allow himself to be distracted by dispersing smoke instead of putting out the fire.

“Do not forget your role and purpose: You are an educator and educators are concerned with correcting errors and not demonstrating them. So, how excellent you would be, for example, if you are able to develop the religious state of the student without making him feel that he is negligent, a wrongdoer, sinful and heedless ... Do not be like those who forget their role and purpose and consequently pay their greatest attention to pointing out the error instead of correcting it.

“Would you like that for your sister!?” ... The concern of the educator must not be confined to solving the outward problem.

Rather, he must search for its origins and root them out. That is because that which is outwardly apparent to us only reflects the effects of the problem and not its true or full reality.

“When correcting the error, you may need to employ direct confrontation. There is no problem with that but remember that this step on many occasions may represent the last step. That is because demonstration, generalisation, pointing out, silence of discontent and jesting are all tools that can be employed first prior to the open and frank confrontation.

“O Abu Dharr, you are weak, and it is a trust, and it will be a cause of disgrace and remorse on the Day of Judgement except for the one who discharges its right fully” ... The educator may need to use frankness instead of flattery, as it can often get to the point and be effective especially when it is utilised at the appropriate time.

“On many occasions the silence of the educator accompanied by a type of smile carrying an element of censure has a greater impact in respect to guiding others than direct speech and rebuke. Indeed, the Messenger of Allah ﷺ utilised that: “The smile indicating discontent”.

“One of the children said to his friend: “My father doesn’t hit us, however his severe glances and harsh words to us when we fall into error are more severe than being hit”. Comment: Punishment without doubt represents a successful educational and raising tool, however, it is not necessary for the only form of punishment to be a beating that afflicts physical pain.

“Styles of punishment include: 1) The stern look, 2) Praising someone else in front of him, 3) Depriving, 4) Avoidance, 5) Threat of punishment, 6) Giving extra homework, 7) Reprimanding and expressing disapproval, 8) Ear pulling and 9) Hitting.

“I regard punishments in Tarbiyah (educational raising) to be like a diversion, where we get off the path for it, to then return to the path after it has ended. The shorter and clearer it is the better” Dr Abdul Karim Bakkar.

“When we punish at the time of anger, that could lead us to being excessive in the punishment and to possibly making an error when attempting to treat an error. However, when we delay the punishment until we are clam, we will be closer to what is right and wise. When we are stern at such a time, then we will be stern because it is our calm mind that commands us to be so and not our raging emotions.

“Even though hitting is considered to be one of the tools of Tarbiyah (educational raising), for it to be considered as an educational hitting it must not be violent or harmful, it must be far from the face, be undertaken in the most minimised manner and only for the major errors. It must also be the last tool utilised in educational raising and not the first.

“Educationally raising children does not mean constant softness and kindness. Parents may require resoluteness and firmness on occasions. Continuous softness is harmful just like continuous harshness. If someone from his family members did something wrong the Messenger of Allah ﷺ use to sometimes avoid them until they had repented.

“When you are a successful educator, you make use of the errors of the student and transform them into gains in respect to aiding your educational evaluation of him. Remember that many of the major transitions in the lives of people occurred as a result of an error which they did well in benefitting from in a particular manner!

“One of the Sahabah (companions) cursed a man due to his repeated drinking of alcohol. Then the Messenger of Allah ﷺ said: “Don’t curse him, for verily he loves Allah and His Messenger”. The successful educator is the one who does his best to separate between the error and the one who committed the error. That is because those who fall into some bad matters are not always bad and the ability to extract the positive aspects from those who people see as being bad reflects a skill possessed by optimistic educators.

“There is no problem on occasions to practise the role of a dumb person in the process of detecting the errors of others. That is because questing for the errors of other people with skill and intelligence does involve a kind of stupidity. That is when he conceals the intelligence by feigning ignorance of these errors accompanied by the calm and covert attempt to treat them.

“Included among the practical means to decrease the dangers of the internet for our children, is to continuously provide them with good internet sites, to place the computer in an open place in the house, to put a time limit upon internet usage, to disconnect it during the late hours of the night, to make use of internet safety programmes and to increase within them the awareness that Allah is always watching and fully aware.

“A heated argument took place between a boy and his brother, and during it, the boy crossed the limits of manners. This represents an opportunity for us to teach the practice of apology to the one who did wrong and forgiveness to the one who was wronged. That is in addition to teaching ourselves self-control, fairness and impartiality. In this way we transform the errors of those around us into real opportunities to impart education and guidance.

Study and Education

“It is important for us not to register our children at a particular school just because it is the closest to our house. For our children to accomplish a distinguished study attainment a suitable school consisting of competent teachers must be chosen, even if that burdens us more in terms of expenses and travelling distance.

“Just as praying in the first row prepares the one performing the prayer to interact with and focus upon what the Imam is reciting, similarly the student sitting in a front position of the study hall has a positive impact upon his concentration and attainment, just as it increases his interaction and active participation with what the teacher is delivering.

“It is important that our children have a love inside themselves to go to school. That can be accomplished by: Purchasing all the child’s study supplies or stationary in a special manner, setting the child’s goal from the beginning of the year, like for him to be in the top five of the class for example, setting short-term incentives and rewards for the child, on a monthly basis for example, through continual encouragement and by reducing the amount of criticism and laying blame.

“It is very important when we tell our children off for falling short in a particular subject not to forget to praise them for their excellence in the other subjects. That is because telling them off for a short coming or deficiency in the absence of praise for success could lead to frustration or feelings of despair.

“Allah, the Most Majestic and High, linked the whole Dunya (life of this world) with an objective to be fulfilled from it. He said:

﴿أَفَحَسِبْتُمْ أَنَّمَا خَلَقْنَاكُمْ عَبَثًا﴾

«Then did you think that We created you uselessly ?»[Al-Muminun: 115]

Similarly, it would be beneficial for us to continually make a goal for our children which they strive and focus upon reaching. That is because there is a major difference between a child who studies because his goal is to become a doctor, engineer, teacher or pilot, and a child who studies merely because his family have asked him to, as he would then treat it with a lack of purpose, seriousness and indifference.

“It is important to increase the enthusiasm of our children towards the new academic year by providing incentives, encouragement and rewards, so that our children go to study upon the basis of a love and wanting, and not the basis of compulsion and coercion. That is because the strong beginning has a major impact upon the rest of the days of the year.

“Concern with purchasing good quality school items for our children in terms of bags, pens and clothes amongst others, increases the enthusiasm of our children to study. The child by his nature always compares between himself and his classmates and we are required to meet the needs of our children without being excessive or going over the top. The Prophet ﷺ said: “Had Usamah been a girl, I would have adorned and dressed him up until I married him off”.

“The Messenger of Allah ﷺ: “Every one of you is a shepherd and every one of you is responsible for his flock” ... The sensation of the teacher that the father is concerned with his son due to his repeated visits to the school or the comments he leaves in his son’s work books, increases the enthusiasm of the teacher to have concern for that son, just as it increases the son’s pride for his father in front of his classmates, whilst the opposite produces the opposite results.

“The father took a piece of paper and wrote a letter on it addressed to his son’s teachers thanking them and offering his continuous cooperation with them. In this way the father can generate good relations with them, and its impact also returns directly to his son in the school.

“From among the matters which make the teacher loved and impactful among his students: Quickly memorising the names of the students, balanced joking, talking about some personal experiences, respecting the students and not acting in an authoritative and superior manner.

“Primary education is from the most important stages of education as it reflects the foundation upon which the building is established. Many people do not provide it with its right level of appreciation and concern! “If the primary school teacher is weak, he will not be rectified by the strength of the secondary school teacher or university lecturer” Ali At-Tantawi.

“An argument started between two groups of the Sahabah (Prophet’s companions). The news of that reached the Messenger of Allah ﷺ and so he occupied them all in work that took up all their time until they calmed down and forget their disagreement. Comment: Listening a lot to the complaints of quarrelling people can sometimes increase them and problems only increase in number when the amount of free or idle time increases.

“It is important for parents to save a set portion of their income for the purpose of securing a better education for their children in the future. That is because children attaining the best certifications from the best universities represents a great gift and permanent benefit that parents provide to their children.

“Statistics indicate to a major deterioration in the level of education in many third-world countries. This calls for parents to cover that deficiency by making their children acquire a variety of skills and enrolling them in training and language courses.

﴿وَلَلْآخِرَةُ خَيْرٌ لَّكَ مِنَ الْأُولَىٰ ٤﴾

«And the Hereafter is better for you than the first [life]» [Adh-Dhuha: 4]

“Being concerned about the certifications of our children, their grades and excelling in their studies is an essential matter. However, are we concerned to the same level or to an even greater level with their prayer, friends, and behavioural conduct?!

“It is a mistake to only confine the education to what our children learn in their schools alone. Rather, we must develop their culture and minds through numerous readings, cultural programmes, beneficial discussions and games that stimulate their minds.

"So that you don't reinforce jealousy" ... People are naturally inclined to the love of wanting exclusive possession. In student atmospheres, the spirit of competition is elevated to reach undesirable levels. The educator may have a negative role in that without sensing or being aware of that. That occurs due to the excessive concern he gives to some students or his unjustified neglect of others.

"Accommodation is essential" ... The forms of competition with the student are numerous, in the case where it begins with an attempt by the student to appear in the best form before the educator until it reaches the point of the student attempting to gain exclusiveness to the teacher at the expense of his classmates. When confronted by that, the educator needs a high level of skill which allows him to distribute his concern in a balanced manner. There is also no problem in respect to the justified preference, in view of an evident distinction or high level of responsiveness, just like the situation of the Prophet ﷺ with some of his Sahabah (companions).

"So that you don't lose your students" ... When the differentiation is unjustified, then this raises the level of sensitivity and jealousy from one angle, just as it could lead to a coldness in the relationship or indeed, perhaps, to the teacher losing many of his students and receiving harsh criticism in relation to his objectivity and fairness!

“It was for this reason that the Ansar were angered when they were unaware of the secret of the Prophet’s ﷺ giving preference to other than them in respect to the war booty.

“The successful holiday is not is not judged by how much money we spend on it, but rather the one in which we attain the greatest rest, break and relaxation. Our success in respect to accomplishing enjoyable holidays for our children which are far removed from extravagant spending and squandering represents a success for our Deen and our Dunya (life of this world).

Seasonal Messages

"It is important to make our children participate with us in some actions of goodness during Ramadan. So, for example, we can take them with us sometimes to perform the Tarawih prayer, we can send them out to give charity to the poor, and we can recite with them daily, even if it is only some verses of the Qur'an. That is because actions have a greater impact than words.

"There is no problem if the parents give a gift to the children for every part or collection of parts of the Qur'an that they read during Ramadan. Then when they hand over the gift to them, they remind them that their gift with Allah is greater, because He, Glorified be He, is the Most Magnificent and Greatest.

"In the world of football, even the good player needs to practise and train before the match starts. The dispositional (mental and emotional) preparation for Ramadan and setting a defined goal to be accomplished during it, helps us to take advantage of it in the best possible manner.

"When we implant Iman (belief) within ourselves and within those we are responsible for, we are in truth participating in solving many of the problems that we suffer from. That is because the correct attachment to the Deen (i.e. Islam) constantly pushes its possessor towards that which is better and the seasons of goodness represent a golden opportunity for that.

"When Ramadan arrived, the Prophet ﷺ used to say: "Verily, this month has come to you, and in it there is a night that is better than a thousand months. Whoever is deprived of it is deprived of all goodness, and no one is deprived of its goodness except the one who is truly deprived". From the very first night, the educator alerts to the most important prize of this month, "Laylat ul-Qadr" (The Night of Power/Decree), so that its preparation can be completed early.

"Pressing our children to perform the recommended acts of worship like the Tarawih prayers besides other acts, could lead to discouraging them from undertaking them or to them performing them with great dislike. Instead, utilising convincing arguments, a gradual approach, leading by example and good companionship, represent the best ways to educating and raising them upon that.

"When we go over the top in respect to our desire for our children to fast until the time of sunset and on all days of Ramadan, we may be raising them upon the dislike of fasting and even the dislike of Ramadan itself!

"A practical lesson" ... The mother decided for the Iftar on that day to be very limited and without a large main meal. When the children enquire about that, she informs them that they have Muslim brothers who do not even have what is much less than what they have upon the table.

"Ramadan is not a month of being on holiday from work, activity and normal living. This is corroborated by the Messenger ﷺ having cohabited with three of his wives during Ramadan in the third year after Hijrah and by the battles of Badr and Al-Khandaq (the trench), which were the first and last battles with Quraish, also taking place during the month of Ramadan.

“There is an important benefit in the story of Nuh with his son and that is that the Tawfiq (attainment and success) with guidance is in the hands of Allah. Regardless of how great our care, concern and means were in respect to our education and raising of our children, we cannot guarantee the result. This makes us persist upon supplicating to Allah to grant our children Tawfiq (success) in respect to the attainment of goodness, and to undertake that especially in the best times and places.

﴿وَٱلۡفَجۡرِ ١ وَلَيَالٍ عَشۡرٖ ٢﴾

«By the dawn(1) And [by] ten nights(2)» [Al-Fajr: 1-2]

“Just as our children feel the difference between Ramadan and other months in terms of worship and conduct, we must also make them feel the difference between the last ten nights of it and the nights that proceed them, because, in short, they are the best nights in the life of this world.

“Better than one thousand nights” ... The father declared a daily competition to his children to be successful on Laylat ul-Qadr (The Night of Power). So, at the end of every night, he asks his children: “What righteous action are you competing with to be successful on this night?” In this manner, the father can motivate himself and his children throughout the last ten days of Ramadan.

“Popular proverbs can break down some educational concepts that we want to realise within those we are educating and raising. For example, the saying: “The purebred horse races or chases the next (to the finish line)”. This acts as an encouragement to intensify one's efforts whenever the end of something approaches. This applies to the acts of worship at the end of Ramadan and it was stated in the reported tradition: "Verily, the actions are only (evaluated) by the last and final acts".

"The scholars have mentioned that the last ten nights are better than their days. Therefore, whoever is compelled to purchase necessities or fulfil some need with his children, then he should do that during the daytime of Ramadan so that he can dedicate his nights in acts of worship and be facilitated for that. That will be by his family not spending too much time shopping due to their fasting and their being educated upon the magnitude of those nights.

"Each of you is a shepherd and each of you is responsible for his flock" ... It is not right that the father and mother are dedicated to fasting and standing in prayer at night whilst the markets and streets are designated to their children! As such, accompanying the children to the Masajid during the last ten nights and even if only to complete some of the Tarawih and night prayers, is better than performing them all without them, just as it is an opportunity to strengthen the Iman within them.

﴿وَٱلۡمُسۡتَغۡفِرِينَ بِٱلۡأَسۡحَارِ ١٧﴾

«and those who seek forgiveness before dawn(17)» [Al-i'Imran: 17]

"The times before dawn represent an amazing opportunity for the parents to sit down in a tranquil sitting of Iman with the rest of the members of their family, away from the hustle and bustle of visits, invitations, and constantly keeping up with the news and satellite programmes.

“There is an important educational lesson connected to the Du’aa (supplication) that has come specified for Laylat ul-Qadr (The Night of Power/Decree): “O Allah, You are the Pardoner, You love to pardon, so, pardon me”. As such, whoever wishes for Allah to pardon him on that night, should also pardon anyone who has wronged him. That is because the recompense is commensurate with the action (i.e. you get what you give).

“Allah revealed the best of His Books with the best of His Angels upon the best of His Messengers on the best of His months upon the best of His nations: And thus “Laylat ul-Qadr was better than a thousand months”, so, let Allah see from you the best of actions during it.

“The father asked his son: “When should you give the taxi driver his fare?” He answered: “At the completion of the job”. So, the father said: “And the same applies to you until you take your wage in full from Allah. Therefore, complete your task, your worship and Ramadan striving until the very last minute of the month.

“The end of the month came and the people went to withdraw their wages. Then the internal struggle starts between the love of accumulating personal wealth on one hand and giving goodness to people on the other. That is until the believing souls remember the statement of our beloved Al-Mustafa ﷺ: “Wealth is not decreased by (the giving of) Sadaqah (charity)”.

“The educator must not make the falling short of the one he is educating or raising during the first half of Ramadan be a cause to make him despair or be neglectful for the remainder of the month, especially as the remaining part contains that which is better than a thousand months.

“The great concern of the Prophet ﷺ to take advantage of the last ten nights was reflected in that he used to perform Ghusl between Maghrib and ‘Ishaa to invigorate himself as he did not sleep during its nights. He would tighten his waist belt, waken his family members and stay awake praying during the night.

“Is it not intriguing that the best supplication for a Muslim to repeat during the Night of Power (Laylat ul-Qadr) is: “O Allah You are the Pardoner, You love to pardon, so, pardon me!”? It reflects a lesson that however much we have striven in acts of obedience, we still having nothing apart from the pardon of Allah and His Mercy (to rely upon): “No one will ever enter Paradise by his action”.

“There is a lot of talk amongst the people about Laylat ul-Qadr being on a particular night which causes people to abandon making effort in the other nights, a matter which is contrary to the wisdom behind Allah concealing the precise night of Laylat ul-Qadr.

“Al-Qiyam (Standing at night) does not only include the prayers that we can perform during Laylat ul-Qadr. Indeed, cleansing our hearts, forgiving all those who have wronged us and resolving to change our condition after this night are all undertaken for the purpose of worship through which we draw close to Allah during this night.

“When the person feels the dryness of his heart and that it is not being impacted by the Qur’an and standing in night prayer, then he must undertake a host of righteous actions which draw him close to Allah, like the giving of Sadaqah (charity), maintaining familyrelations, pardoning and other such acts. That is because the pleasure attained from the prayer is no more than a reward that Allah gives to the one who has acted well prior to the prayer.

“The constant sinful act of disobedience is the most dangerous of the acts of disobedience upon the person. It is the disobedient act which continues with us even if we have prayed and fasted. It can be like harboring malice and hatred, wronging others and cutting the relations or ties of the womb. It is from the success of the believer to hasten towards repentance after the act of disobedience. If he becomes compulsively attached to it, then that would be a sign of badness and failure.

“An employee worked the whole month. Then when it was time for him to collect his wages, he was absent and did not attend!! The following came stated in the Noble Hadith: “And he will forgive them on the last night of Ramadan”. They asked: “O Messenger of Allah, is it Laylat ul-Qadr?” He said: “No, but the worker only attains his wage when his work has come to an end”. And to Allah belongs the Sublime similitude.

“Making our children accustomed to the voluntary fasts represents an important opportunity to plant a number of wonderful concepts within them. Among them is that the Muslim is someone who has a high ambition and is not satisfied by fulfilling the obligation for the sin to be removed from him. Rather, he draws closer to Allah through recommended acts of obedience until he attains the love of Allah: “And my slave continues to draw close to me by the extra (non-obligatory) acts until I love him”.

﴿قُلْ بِفَضْلِ ٱللَّهِ وَبِرَحْمَتِهِۦ فَبِذَٰلِكَ فَلْيَفْرَحُواْ﴾

«Say, "In the bounty of Allah and in His mercy “in that let them rejoice; it is better than what they accumulate."(58)» *[Yunus: 58]*

“It is good for our children to feel that our joy attached to Eid is no less than our joy attached to the completion of the favour of Allah upon us through the conclusion of fasting the month of favour and mercy.

“It is important to be generous to our wives and children at the time of Eid in emulation of the Prophet ﷺ. However, it is also important to remind them of those poor and destitute Muslims to whom Eid comes whilst they do not possess the means to celebrate. Our children will then be aware of the blessing of Allah upon them, just as the bond of Islamic brotherhood will develop within them.

“It is nice for our children to choose their own Eid clothes with your advice and by persuading them in a kind manner of what is best. This increases their confidence in themselves, builds their personalities and increases their experiences.

“Eid is an opportunity to implant the importance of maintaining the ties of the womb within those we are educating and raising. The child or student will then learn that celebrating Eid is an act of worship which is not completed except by another act of worship and that is visiting, meeting and communicating with family and relatives, whilst leaving behind any prior problems, (remembering the Eid saying): Every year and you are well!

“Just as the prayer and fasting are acts of worship, being generous to wives and children at the time of Eid is an act of worship. Showing joy at Eid is an act of worship, smiling amongst the people is an act of worship, meeting and communicating with friends, neighbours and relatives are all acts of worship.

“Any characteristic transforms into a behaviour and norm when it is repeated for more than twenty days. Therefore, after Ramadan the person is easily able to preserve and maintain his good behavioural conducts.

“The Hajj is not an act of worship that we undertake in order for us to merely fulfil a pillar from the pillars of Islam. Rather, the Hajj is the deal of a lifetime that we contract with Allah.

The cost we pay is:

To control and discipline our conduct and tongues: “He does not use obscene or indecent speech and he does not act sinfully”. To follow the Sunnah in respect to that which we are undertaking: “Adopt your ritual practices from me”. As for what is provided in exchange for this cost, then: “The accepted Hajj has no recompense other than Jannah (Paradise)”.

"The millions of people who go to Hajj from every place and expend their wealth and efforts only expend such difficulty for the sake of Allah desiring His Paradise and fearing His fire. A lesson that we teach students and children is that there is nothing attained without a cost and that the attainment of the most precious Paradise requires the payment of a high price.

"In the vicinity of the Ka'bah the Prophet ﷺ declared his general pardon for his enemies: "Go for you are set free". And from the vicinity of the Ka'bah whilst we are engaged in our Sa'y and our Tawaaf, let us declare our general pardon for all those who have wronged us during the Hajj and prior to it. This represents one of the greatest acts of worship of the hearts which draw us close to Allah for Him to accept our acts from us and pardon us.

"When departing from the Hajj to return to his family, he should be reminded of his final departure from life. When donning his Ihram, he should be reminded of the wearing of his burial shroud. And when he is among the swarming crowds during the Tawaaf and the Sa'y, he should be reminded of the swarming crowds of creation standing before Allah on the Day of Judgement.

"The eighth of Dhu-l-Hijjah is the day of preparation for the great day of Arafat. Just like with the Ihram it is preparation to keep away from the Haram in terms of backbiting, argumentation or indecent speech, and to perform many acts of obedience and the recitation of the Qur'an until the inner self is softened and is ready to supplicate to Allah and communicate with Him during the greatest day specified by Allah.

"Before the setting of the sun during Arafat the Messenger of Allah ﷺ said: "There does not remain from your Dunya (life of this world) in respect to what has already passed by from it except like what remains from this day of yours in respect to what has already passed by from it".

"The day of Arafat is a day of supplication and hope. That is because it is a day of giving from Allah. The Messenger of Allah ﷺ said: "The best supplication is the supplication of the day of Arafat" and he said: "Shaytan does not see a day in which he is more disdained than the day of Arafat". In truth it is not a whole day but rather a few hours that represent the conclusion of the Hajj: "Al-Hajj is Arafat". As such, we lessen anything that occupies us away from Allah during that time, in terms of food, drink and speech.

"I respond to Your call O Allah! I respond to Your call. You have no partner. I respond to Your call.". This represents a self-testimony from the one performing Hajj that his Hajj is for Allah alone and not for the sake of reputation or receiving the praise of others. So, he must remember that every time he utters his response and renews his sincerity and intention until he becomes someone performing the Hajj in truth. That is because not everyone who goes to the Hajj is worthy of being called someone who has performed it!

"A pilgrim goes to perform the Hajj. He then pardons, overlooks, helps, smiles, supplicates and remembers Allah often. That is whilst another pilgrim argues, disputes, gets agitated and angry, reproaches and blames. Are these two equal in the sight Allah?

﴿فَلَا رَفَثَ وَلَا فُسُوقَ وَلَا جِدَالَ فِي ٱلْحَجِّ﴾

«there is [to be for him] no sexual relations and no disobedience and no disputing during Hajj.» *[Al-Baqara: 197]*

"During the night of Jumu'ah it is recommended to send prayers upon the Messenger of Allah ﷺ. When the educator applies that, he will implant the extolling of the Messenger of Allah ﷺ, love for him and awe of him within the one he is educating or raising, and then consequently the strong desire to follow and emulate him.

"Jumu'ah is like the Eid of the week. It is blessed, and similarly, if it is also a day off from work, it represents a right for the wife and children. It is beneficial for them to feel within it a sense of change and renewal through spending it with them, by burning incense in the house and making it fragrant, by wearing the best clothes, relieving the wife of the task of cooking, cancelling personal commitments, taking the children to the Jumu'ah Khutbah (in the Masjid) and to undertake all that which revitalises the activeness of everyone for a week which is full of striving and the determination to accomplish things.

Tarbiyah Mistakes

"The Messenger of Allah ﷺ said: "When Allah loves a people (Qawm) he enters kindness (and gentleness) upon them". Included among the matters which impact negatively upon the realisation of kindness with children, are: Continuously raising the voice, issuing lots of commands and forbiddances and punishing any bad act regardless of how small or insignificant it may be!

"If Islam did not command us to hit the child for leaving the prayer which is the pillar of the Deen if the child has not yet reached ten years of age, then how can some of us hit our young children for mistakes and the naturally occurring naughtiness which is widespread in the behaviour of children?!

"Some parents frighten their children by mentioning the dark, police, thieves and criminals, which is a major Tarbiyah mistake which weakens the self-confidence of the child and perhaps makes him apprehensive, shy and withdrawn.

﴿وَبِٱلْوَٰلِدَيْنِ إِحْسَانًا﴾

«and to parents do good » *[Al-Baqara: 83]*

"A father gives a toy to his child and asks him: "Do you love me?" and so the child answers by saying: "Yes". He then asks him: "Why do you love me?" So, he says: "Because you bought a toy for me". Then the educating father says whilst hugging his son: "No my son, you love me because I am your father". We must educate and raise our children upon loving us because we are their parents and not only because buy them nice things.

“The child said to his mother scared: “I found a mouse as big as an elephant in the bathroom”. The mother then responded saying: “I have told you a million times not to exaggerate!!” On many occasions some may not use the best practise despite being aware of it, and then fall into the error of exaggeration whilst educating and raising children or students to avoid it.

“Included among our mistakes is that when our children come to us with their school results, we criticise the low grades in some subjects, whilst we forget to praise them for their distinction in other subjects! The Messenger of Allah ﷺ said: “What an excellent servant Abdullah is! If only he were to perform prayer during the night”. Abdullah said: “I never left the performance of the night prayer after that”. As such, praise paves the way for the acceptance of criticism.

“That person is better than so and so person” or “So and so is cleverer than you”. From among the mistakes that we fall into is the many comparisons we make between our children and others. That is because Allah did not make the minds of people the same and exaggerating in the use of comparisons could lead to despair or cultivate a heightened level of jealousy.

“Mothers are delighted when a child is quiet and complain when the child is restlessness. That is whilst the mischief of the child could be indicative of the child’s intelligence and vitality which needs to be developed and directed, rather than be countered and suppressed.

"Some parents not only deprive their children of the blessing of supplicating for them but rather add to that the calamity of supplicating against them! The Messenger of Allah ﷺ said: "Do not invoke curses on yourselves, your children, and your property, lest you happen to do it at an hour during which Allah is not asked for anything except that He grants it".

"If the guidance of the educator contradicts his action, then his guidance would not have the least amount of impact. He would be like someone who is holding a pen in one hand and an eraser in the other hand. Then every time he writes something with his right hand, his left hand erases it!

"Some fathers cast the responsibility of the Tarbiyah upon their wives based on the argument of them being preoccupied outside of the house! This is a common error as Tarbiyah is a task that is completed by both parents together, where each has a role not performed by the other.

"Excessively commanding and forbidding the children leads to them becoming unresponsive to their parents and could even teach them to fall into disobedience without them being aware of it. It came related from the Messenger of Allah ﷺ that he said: "Help your children upon righteous conduct. Whoever wishes extracts the (source of) disobedience for his child".

"Many have spoken about the danger of servants from numerous angles. However, it is enough for us to know that studies have shown that 60% of servants in the Gulf states are non-Muslims! Just as many of the Muslim servants are not practising Islam!

“The severe insistence, pressure and compulsion placed upon our children to perform the prayer before the age of ten could foster within them a dislike and aversion towards it after that.

“Remember a day when you decided such and such a matter” ... Failing to forget the mistake of the one you are educating or raising and continuously condemning him for it is a major error. It has authentically been related from the Messenger of Allah ﷺ that he said: “If one of your slave women commits Zina (fornication) and her perpetration is established by clear evidence, then lash her with the Hadd (prescribed punishment) and do not hurl statements of condemnation against her”.

“Major effects which are the result of being harsh with children include: Disturbed dreams, loss of self-confidence, resistance, a weak love for the parents, an aggressive personality, a weak personality, weak social relationships and becoming habituated to receiving punishment.

“Keep your mind on the alert”, “Don’t let them play or take advantage of you”, “Keep vigilant” ... These are the types of statements that we repeat to our children out of fear that they will fall into weakness among their friends. However, if we do this a lot, it could teach and develop within them selfishness, egoism, thinking badly of others, resistance to making concessions or overlooking anything, and playing with or using deceptive ploys with other people.

“Mockery, sharp criticism and continuous reproach demolishes the person’s emotional and mental self, whether he is a child or adult. This makes him feel frustration, hopelessness, weak confidence in himself and in his ability to succeed.

"The Messenger of Allah ﷺ said: "The eye (i.e. evil envious eye) is truth", however, some people go over the top in respect to linking many occurrences and incidents to the "evil eye" in an erroneous and mistaken manner, and consequently have a bad view of anyone who looks at their child in an impressed or admiring manner.

﴿وَقُل لِّعِبَادِى يَقُولُوا۟ ٱلَّتِى هِىَ أَحْسَنُ﴾

«And tell My servants to say that which is best» *[Israel: 53]*

"Sometimes we forget that children have feelings which must also be taken into consideration. That is because we tell our children off in front of people, relatives, and colleagues, which represents one of our most common mistakes related to dealing with mistakes.

"You're driving me crazy", "You don't understand", "Stupid", "Shaytan (devil)" ... These are inappropriate statements which are repeated by some parents towards their children and have a negative impact upon both parties: The parents as these negative statements reflect their mental and emotional dispositions and their view towards their children, and the children who decrease their value of themselves and thereby dare to undertake the mistake and repeat it, because they are convinced that they are devils and stupid.

“In the market the child looks at a toy and asks his father to buy it for him. The father refuses and the child repeats his request once more, however, the father refuses again. The child then begins to cry, the father gets embarrassed and then buys the child what he wants. The message that settles within the child as a result of that is: Crying is the best way to get everything that I want!

“It is not correct to hide our apparent faults in front of those we are educating or raising by way of pretence. Rather, it is important that we appear before them just as we are. If we are embarrassed of the large number of our faults, then the solution is to remedy them whilst it is not to hide them and provide the false appearance of perfection.

“The statement: “You are young” creates a generation of people old in years but young in aspirations and weak in resolve. That is because the one who always feels that he is young will never think for himself and be innovative. Rather, he will keep repeating the same mistakes time and time again and will continue to always fall short. He will then excuse himself with the excuse of still being young!

“Close the door”, “Bring me the key”, “Turn the TV on”, “Bring me water” ... Making many unnecessary requests could lead to the children being disgruntled. It may also lead to indifference towards these requests or to them being undertaken with a lot of disgruntlement and grumbling.

“From the unfortunate matters is that many fathers are nicer, calmer and more playful with the people, whilst they deprive their children and wives of that altogether. That is whilst we must be aware that the person's dealing with his family represents the true test of his moral behaviour and manners. The Prophet ﷺ said: "The best of you is the one who is best to his Ahl (wives, family) and I am the best of you to my Ahl (wives, family)".

"My son is stupid", "My children have weak capabilities", "He has no right to study" ... If the one responsible for educating and raising is not greatly convinced in the student's or child's ability to elevate and develop, then he will never be able to raise him a lot.

"One of the mistakes that some parents fall into when the child makes some errors is to threaten him by saying that Allah will punish him and enter him into the fire of hell. This is a really big error and reflects a misconception which the student or child should not be educated or raised upon. That is because he is not legally responsible and accountable in origin and there is no reward or punishment in respect to him. It may also settle within him that Allah, Glorified be He the Most High, is only a source of punishment and fire, thereby weakening love for Him within his heart.

"Some mothers, due to the great fear they have for their children, transform into mothers who are always worried, anxious and on edge. However, the mother must always keep in mind that the hearts of her children are in Allah's hand and not hers. It is He alone who is the One who guides and grants success, whilst it is her right to live her life even if her children have not turned out as she wished:

﴿فَلَعَلَّكَ بَٰخِعٞ نَّفۡسَكَ عَلَىٰٓ ءَاثَٰرِهِمۡ إِن لَّمۡ يُؤۡمِنُواْ بِهَٰذَا ٱلۡحَدِيثِ أَسَفًا ٦﴾

«Then perhaps you would kill yourself through grief over them, [O Muhammad], if they do not believe in this message, [and] out of sorrow(6)» *[Al-Kahf: 6]*

"Treating technology, like the internet and satellite channels, as being evil and our children's enemy, will never benefit us at all. Rather, we must be aware that modern technology has become a reality which we must invest in and seek benefit from in terms of its positives, instead of failing in our attempts to isolate our children from it.

"The mother's extra concern for everything to be ok whilst picking up on every error and showing her displeasure in it, combined with the issuing of many commands and forbiddances, leads to disturbing the home atmosphere and to the children becoming restless, due to their inability to attain the satisfaction of the mother. This, in turn, could lead to weakening the concern for her feelings and their kindness and dutifulness towards her.

"If you are not a good source of humour and joviality, then be someone who receives them well. That is because those of thick blood cannot be influential and loved among others, even if they were their fathers or mothers. Anas bin Malik said: "The Messenger of Allah ﷺ was the most jovial of people".

"A big mistake we make when responding to the demands of our children is when we say "In Shaa' Allah" (If Allah wills) and then after that we fail to implement those demands! In this way we unintentionally raise them upon disliking connecting matters to the will of Allah Glorified be He, The Most High.

"Our children are not us. When we insist upon imposing our convictions, thoughts and experiences upon them, we are making a major error. That is because we must raise our children for a time which is not our own time.

"Children feeling that no matter what they do they will never attain the satisfaction of their parents due to them constantly being told off and not being encouraged and praised, makes them feel despair and perhaps makes them become deficient in respect to the kindness, dutifulness, respect and appreciation they provide.

"Stinginess has a variety of forms, the most well-known form of stinginess relates to money, however, one of its most severe kinds is the stinginess in relation to giving constant commendation, praise and encouragement.

"Going over the top in any matter ruins it. As such, going over the top in respect to praising the child leads to spoiling, going over the top in respect to telling the child off leads to fear and indifference, going over the top in terms of spending leads to over reliance, going over the top in respect to paying attention to mistakes leads to weariness, and going over the top in relation to fearing for the children leads to introversion and the inability to face the realities of life.

"The child tries to gain the attention of his parents by throwing his food on the ground. His mother calls out: "Don't do that, son". He stops for a bit and then after a minute he repeats the same behaviour. In this way the mother is giving him what he wants in terms of attention! This type of behaviour then becomes a norm for the child.

"The Messenger of Allah ﷺ forbade that a man should come to his family like (an unexpected) night visitor doubting their loyalty and searching for their flaws". Comment: Searching for the faults or flaws of others and lying in wait for them has no place at all in education and raising, even if that was done under the pretext of rectifying and giving direction!

"Our great eagerness for those around us to excel makes us forget that it is from the nature of the human to make errors as well as to get things right. This makes us in a state of continuously and repeatedly laying blame until the very people who are closest to us become fed up of us and annoyed at us.

"The educator loses the person before him when he deals with him upon the basis that he is better and purer than him. That is as the true educator is the closest, most beloved and sincere in respect to giving goodness to the person before him. This is what makes him the best and purest in the sight of others.

"Our great eagerness for others to not fall into error and for us to present our opinions and advice in every matter; large or small, marginalises the personalities of those we are guiding and transforms them into followers and imitators, not leaders who use their own initiative.

"The educator can lose in an hour of anger all that he has built over a period of many months and years. That is because the sharp personal insult is engraved in the heart of its victim and he may not forget it for the duration of his life. It is for this reason that the Prophet ﷺ forbade striking the face due to what that signifies in terms of immense insult.

“Smoking is a main cause of heart disease, lung disease and the thickening of the arteries” ... It is a strange contradiction that we find this written upon a packet of cigarettes itself! It is an example of the contradiction that we practise when we forbid our children from the Haram (prohibited acts) whilst at the same time facilitating for them the means to reach it, by providing for them unrestricted access to the internet, lots of money, free time and access to bad company!

“When we threaten our children a lot without implementing that which we are threatening them with, then we are saying to them indirectly that it is ok for them not to listen to what we say and to not implement our commands! This should make us not threaten them unless it is with that which we are sure and resolved that we will implement.

“The educator is not a radar device, the function of which is to pick up on all mistakes in order to rectify them. That is as one of the ways of correcting some mistakes is to turn a blind eye to them and overlook them. Otherwise, the educator turns into an unbearable tiresome personality.

“We are overjoyed with our clever and excelling child and so he takes our love and interest. But don’t forget that our child who is less intelligent and weaker in terms of capabilities is in greater need of our caretaking, time, and encouragement.

“To raise the level of our speech with our children we must: Abandon exaggeration as most parents don’t lie but do exaggerate, reduce the amount of swearing oaths, not compare the child to an animal, supplicate a lot during speech, set aside ill-mannered joking, not shout, reduce the speed of our speech and reduce the utilisation of words like “I, in my opinion, I like, I don’t like”.

“It is essential not to dig up the old mistakes of others. Rather, we should overlook and forget them. That is because maintaining the negative perception of others due to their old mistakes prompts them to repeat them and not abandon them.

“Parents get very scared when they see their young children lying. However, the matter should not be over complicated because the child before the age of six years does not lie in an intentional manner but rather the true reality is mixed with his wide imagination.

“Favouritism of parents towards one child over another is a major cause for planting seeds of discord between them in the future, just as it could lead to the rebelliousness of the child when he grows up. Above that, it is also a great wrong perpetrated against the one who is most deserving of mercy from among the people.

“The Sahabah (companions of the Prophet ﷺ) asked a young shepherd about the number of the army of Quraish which passed by him but he didn’t know and so they beat him. The Prophet ﷺ then asked him: “How many camels did they slaughter” and he answered: “Between nine and ten”. Then he ﷺ said: “They are between 900 and 1000 in number". Comment: It is a mistake to deal with the child as if he understands in the same way an adult does and then hold him to account just as we would hold them to account. That is because when the boy was unable to estimate the number of the polytheists (of Quraish), the Prophet ﷺ simplified the matter for him and asked him about the number of camels that they were eating. He was then able to answer and the objective was accomplished.

"Our extra fear over our children and our eagerness to provide them with everything turns into an obstacle in the way of their progression and elevation. It makes them spoiled children who are incapable of bearing responsibility and don't have major goals and high ambitions.

"Beware to not throw the one you are educating or raising into the sea with his hands tied and then ask him not to drown. Your request for a student or child to carry a particular responsibility must be in harmony with their capabilities, concerning which you are meant to be one of the most significant of those who participated and continue to participate in generating with them.

"It is important not to constantly threaten our children by saying that if they don't do such and such, we will not like them. Rather, we could say that "We don't like a certain mistake" instead of saying "We don't like them".

"Nothing kills a person's personality like the constant criticism of everything they do. Those who are accustomed to dealing out constant criticism are not loved and cannot be influential with those they are criticising, even if their criticism is correct and sound.

"The teacher asked her student: "What do you want to be when you grew up?" She answered: "I want to become a teacher so that I can hit your child just like you hit me!" Children have sensitive feelings and their memories hold on to happy and painful memories more than we can imagine.

"Our children differentiate well between the tasks we charge them with from the angle of training them upon carrying responsibility, like receiving the guest and negotiation in buying and selling, on the one hand, and the tasks which we charge them with as a result of our own laziness and fleeing from our responsibilities, on the other hand, like our repeated requests for trivial things that we can easily undertake ourselves, like bringing a cup of tea besides us!

"A father asks his child: "Do you love me more or Mama?" And the mother asks her child: "Do you love me more or Baba?" The thing which both fail to comprehend is that by doing that they are placing their child as if he is faced with two disputing sides where he must take the side of one over the other. This could then have a negative impact upon his mental and emotional disposition and his family security.

"A person naturally inclines towards making his behaviour in harmony with the people's view towards him. As such, constantly reminding people of their mistakes makes them captives to them and incapable of changing them, which is the opposite to what we expect from the constant attention provided to changing the error and rectifying it.

“It is natural that children will argue with each other and even hit each other, however it is not natural for us to get agitated with every small problem that occurs between our children.

“The stressed or tense personality is a personality which constantly criticises, is alarmed by matters, pessimistic, fears the future, possesses an increased level of seriousness which deprives it and those around it of a smile and playfulness, has superficial relationships with others and is therefore a constant source of unease for them. It represents a failed teaching and raising personality, even if it manifests with the appearance of the one who is always concerned and interested.

“Focusing in Tarbiyah upon one aspect and not another; like work at the expense of the family, study at the expense of social relationships, or the Dunya (life of this world) at the expense of the Deen, produces a successful personality which hides behind it many aspects of failure. This is what we can call a fake success!

“An unfortunate matter is for us to turn our virtues into vices. That is when we make use of our children as a platform to boast over other people’s children through making comparisons in which we attempt to prove that our children are always better. It is like we are saying to others: You are not as good as us at raising your children!

“The harsh punishment for an incorrect effort does not only destroy the spirit of initiative but can also perhaps destroy the personality of that person who has made effort as well.

“If you are from those who suffice themselves with theoretical instruction alone, then I suggest to you to choose a child of about ten years of age to cast your thoughts and guidance upon his ears. For sure, he will be very capable of memorising what you want, even if it does not settle in him or is not applied!

“An equation which you desire but is impossible to accomplish is when you pursue every act and every opinion of those you are educating, so as to add to them or to subtract from them, and then after that demand from that person to show initiative and be creative!

“It is hard for me to imagine an educator who kills the spirit of initiative among those he is educating by continuously searching for their mistakes. However, unfortunately, I see this a lot from those undertake this very role when they attempt to allude to perfection and the best form of how matters should be, whilst forgetting the encouragement and motivation for that which has been completed and already happened!

“How do you expect a particular person to undertake a certain initiative when you have blocked him from all entry points to the initiative by issuing explicit instructions and orders in respect to its smallest details, thereby leaving no room for self-exertion and creativity to be made in and upon it!

www.ingramcontent.com/pod-product-compliance
Ingram Content Group UK Ltd.
Pitfield, Milton Keynes, MK11 3LW, UK
UKHW021407190726
13845UKWH00028B/929

9 789366 084121